GURPS® Ⓣ

MODULAR CUTTER

WORKHORSE OF THE IMPERIUM

By **ANDY AKINS**
AND
LOREN WISEMAN

Based on the award-winning Traveller science fiction universe by **MARC MILLER**

Edited by
ANDREW HACKARD AND GENE SEABOLT

Additional material by
TOM BONT, ANDREW BROWN, KURT BROWN, BRANDON COPE, NELSON CUNNINGHAM, JULIEAN GALAK, BOB KONDRK, AND CHRISTOPHER THRASH.

Illustrated by **JESSE DEGRAFF AND ZACH HOWARD**

Deck plans by **ANDY AKINS**

Cover by **RICK ACHBERGER, JESSE DEGRAFF, AND ALEX FERNANDEZ**

GURPS System Design ▌ STEVE JACKSON
Managing Editor ▌ ALAIN H. DAWSON
GURPS Line Editor ▌ SEAN PUNCH
GURPS Traveller Line Editor ▌ LOREN K. WISEMAN
Production Manager ▌ RUSSELL GODWIN
Page Design ▌ JACK ELMY
Production Artist ▌ JEREMY ZAUDER
Production Assistance ▌ ALEX FERNANDEZ
Print Buying ▌ SHAWN HAVRANEK
Art Direction ▌ PHILIP REED
GURPS Errata Coordinator ▌ ANDY VETROMILE
Sales Manager ▌ ROSS JEPSON

Playtesters: Tom Bont, John Buston, Brandon Cope, Charles Hensley, Anthony Jackson, Jim MacLean, Shawn Penrod, Robert Prior, Jeff Stone, Christopher Thrash, and Bolie Williams.

ISBN 1-55634-436-8   1 2 3 4 5 6 7 8 9 10

STEVE JACKSON GAMES

Contents

DECK PLANS

About GURPS

Steve Jackson Games is committed to full support of the *GURPS* system. Our address is SJ Games, Box 18957, Austin, TX 78760. Please include a self-addressed, stamped envelope (SASE) any time you write us! Resources now available include:

Pyramid (**www.sjgames.com/pyramid**). Our online magazine includes new rules and articles for *GURPS*. It also covers the hobby's top games – *Advanced Dungeons & Dragons, Traveller, World of Darkness, Call of Cthulhu, Shadowrun,* and many more – and other Steve Jackson Games releases like *In Nomine, INWO, Car Wars, Toon, Ogre Miniatures,* and more. *Pyramid* subscribers also have access to playtest files online, to see (and comment on) new books before release.

New supplements and adventures. *GURPS* continues to grow, and we'll be happy to let you know what's new. A current catalog is available for an SASE. Or check out our Web site (below).

Errata. Everyone makes mistakes, including us – but we do our best to fix our errors. Up-to-date errata sheets for all *GURPS* releases, including this book, are available from SJ Games; be sure to include an SASE. Or download them from the Web – see below.

Q&A. We strive to answer any game question accompanied by an SASE.

Gamer input. We value your comments, for new products as well as updated printings of existing titles!

Internet. Visit us on the World Wide Web at **www.sjgames.com** for an online catalog, errata, updates, and much more. We also have Compuserve and AOL conferences. *GURPS* has its own Usenet group, too: rec.games.frp.gurps.

GURPSnet. This e-mail list hosts much of the online discussion of *GURPS*. To join, mail majordomo@io.com with "subscribe GURPSnet-L" in the message body, or point your Web browser to **gurpsnet.sjgames.com/**.

The *GURPS Traveller Modular Cutter* Web page is located at **www.sjgames.com/gurps/traveller/modularcutter/**.

Page References

Any page reference that begins with a B refers to *GURPS Basic Set, Third Edition Revised;* e.g., p. B144 refers to page 144 of *Basic Set.* CI refers to *Compendium I,* GT to *GURPS Traveller, Second Edition,* T:FT to *Traveller Far Trader,* and VE to *Vehicles, Second Edition.* For a full list of abbreviations, see p. CI181 or the updated web list at **www.sjgames.com/gurps/abbrevs.html**.

Introduction

The 50-ton modular cutter was one of the first vessels created for the *Traveller* universe, and it has long captured the imagination of players and designers alike. Its unrivaled versatility, utility, and overall performance explain why so many *Traveller* starships – from the *Broadsword*-class mercenary cruiser to the *Donosev*-class survey vessel – have carried one or more of the handy little vessels . . . and why fans of the *Traveller* universe have wanted more information about this jack of all trades.

This book provides that information, with a history of the 50-ton modular cutter and greater detail on its operation. *GURPS Traveller: Modular Cutter* is the first *Traveller* supplement to examine this small craft in detail.

In addition, the following pages describe a wide variety of alternate modular vessels, and dozens of modules to expand their usefulness. More than 70 deck plans illustrate this wealth of vehicles and modules.

The definitive guide to the workhorses of the Imperium, *GURPS Traveller: Modular Cutter* brings the classic 50-ton modular cutter and its many brethren to life.

ABOUT THE AUTHOR

Andy Akins has been a *Traveller* fan since 1979, when he picked up an unassuming black box at his local game shop. Over the years he has contributed art and material to a number of roleplaying books, including deck plans for several *GURPS Traveller* products. A graduate of Iowa State University in computer science, he pays the bills as a computer programmer for a small company as well as by teaching at a local community college. Having grown up in several different places, Andy now lives in central Iowa with his wife and two children. His interests include gaming, computers, movies, astronomy, and anything his children are interested in.

ABOUT THE LINE EDITOR

Loren Wiseman was one of the founding partners of GDW, Inc., original publishers of *Traveller,* and spent more than 20 years there as a game designer, developer, typesetter, and editor. After GDW closed, Loren freelanced for a time, and then came to SJ Games, where he is *Traveller* line editor and expert-in-residence.

JOURNAL OF THE TRAVELLERS' AID SOCIETY

The long-running *Traveller* magazine is now online at **jtas.sjgames.com**, edited by Loren Wiseman. It supports all versions of *Traveller* with news, articles, discussion areas, and reviews. Subscriptions are $15 for a year of weekly updates and full access to archives.

The *Traveller News Service* is updated weekly, chronicling the life and times of the Imperium, and is viewable *free* at **www.sjgames.com/gurps/traveller/news.html**. The SJ Games *Traveller* links page (**www.sjgames.com/gurps/traveller/links.html**) links to the *Traveller* Web Ring, which includes most of the major *Traveller*-oriented websites. For information on subscribing to the *Traveller* mailing list, contact traveller-owner@mpgn.com.

Ling Standard Products began development of the 50-ton modular cutter in 983, during the Third Frontier War. The impetus for the design came from Lucyas hault-Ambon (then an associate vice president in the company's research and development center at Deneb), who perceived a need for a multipurpose utility vessel to support military operations. The lengthy lines of communication involved in interstellar naval campaigns meant that commanders often had to use what vessels were available, regardless of how well-suited they were to the task at hand. Hault-Ambon's inspiration was to create a vessel with specialized features that were interchangeable to a degree never before attempted, and allow one basic small-craft hull to serve many different functions. A fleet could carry a few multipurpose vessels and the appropriate modules in less overall tonnage than the same number of purpose-built vessels. Simply by switching modules, 10 troop transports could be converted to 10 assault landers, and after the assault they could quickly become 10 supply ships for support of the planethead.

The notion of detachable standardized cargo pods was not new – standard containers had been in use on merchant vessels for centuries – and hault-Ambon, during his brief service in the Imperial Navy as a youth, had seen orbital command bases assembled from modular components. While piloting a civilian shuttle pressed into use as a troop transport, hault-Ambon passed several specialized ATV landers sitting idle in a parking orbit. It irritated him that the fleet had to waste so much time commandeering civilian shuttles to do a job that could have been accomplished quicker had the ATV-landing craft been capable of carrying passengers. His inspiration incubated for several years before hatching into the 50-ton modular cutter.

PROTOTYPE

The original design specifications called for three modules: a general cargo module (which could be used as a troop transport by installing detachable seats), an ATV-carrier module, and an assault module (one of the cutter's least successful modules). Three prototype cutters were created at LSP's Deneb construction facility, and company test pilots began to put the vessels through an extensive series of field tests. As a result of the initial tests, several minor design changes were implemented, but the overall results were highly favorable, and a limited production run authorized to produce vessels for inspection by the Imperial Navy. Additional modules were designed (including a fuel skimmer and a weapons pod), but production facilities at Deneb were unable to complete production of the prototypes before the end of the Third Frontier war in 986. The Navy was in no hurry to evaluate the cutter, and it was almost five years before LSP finally received the order to begin production.

Seven Subsequent Miracles

"I don't know who thought up that troop-lander pod, but it was one of the less successful ideas I've ever seen. For those of you who have never seen one, it is basically your standard passenger pod with two enormous scoops fitted to the bottom, which reduced the carrying capacity considerably. The idea was that the cutter would land, dig out entrenchments with the scoops, deposit the troops in the freshly dug position, and then take off. I was one of the military consultants (i.e., discharged soldiers/guinea pigs) hired to field-test the prototype, and we soon nicknamed it SSM, for 'Seven Subsequent Miracles.' This was because several things had to occur in sequence in order for the operation to deposit live troops on the world's surface:

"1. The cutter had to make it to the surface of the world in the face of whatever anti-aircraft fire was active.

"2. The cutter's crew had to locate a suitable spot to land, with a cutter-sized clearing in whatever tree cover was present.

"3. The landing spot had to be a suitable position for an entrenchment, meaning that:

"4. It had to be located in a spot where it would have decent fields of fire, something cutter crews are not very good at discerning.

"5. The soil had to be suitable for rapid excavation by the scoops, no subsurface boulders and the like, and this had to be detectable from a considerable distance in the air.

"6. The troops had to be willing to dive into the entrenchments, sight unseen, trusting in the experience and judgment of the cutter crew to pick a decent spot for someone else to fight from.

"7. The enemy had to be asleep while all of this was going on."

– Between the Lines: A Memoir of the Third Frontier War,
Loston Sato, Captain,
Imperial Marines, retired

Postwar Developments

LSP had intended the cutter for military applications, but the end of the war meant that the Navy would not be buying as many units as the company had initially planned on, and LSP's sales division began looking for other potential markets. At this time, hault-Ambon remembered the massive starbase-construction modules and applied the idea (on a smaller scale) to cutter modules. Designs for self-contained living-quarters modules were followed by modules containing laboratories, medical facilities, administrative offices, and specialized connectors to join the modules together. Orbital or planetary facilities of any size could be constructed simply by transporting the necessary modules to the desired location, and the installation could be moved, expanded, or dismantled with equal ease. This feature brought LSP to the attention of the Imperial Interstellar Scout Service, who contracted the company to build a number of specialized survey modules, and ordered starships such as the *Donosev*-class survey vessel that used modular cutters as their small craft.

Within a decade of its introduction, the 50-ton modular cutter proved to be such a useful design that LSP's production facilities could not produce enough to satisfy demand, and the company licensed production to other concerns. Such is the vessel's penetration in the market that today the word "cutter" is hardly ever used to refer to anything but this particular design of small craft.

Variations on the cutter followed in increasing variety. An armored version of the cutter was developed for frontline military use, followed by a stealth cutter, and ships designed to carry one or more modules into jumpspace.

Today, the modular cutter is seen throughout charted space and beyond, serving an ever-increasing number of needs. Whole industries, and entire planets, depend on the cutter. It is indeed the workhorse of the Imperium.

CHAPTER TWO

Technology and Operations

Modular: adj. 1. Of, pertaining to, or based on a module. 2. Designed with standardized units or dimensions for flexible use.
– *Webster's New College Dictionary*

MODULAR METHODOLOGIES

When appraising modular technologies in the Imperium, most examples fall into one of two categories. The most commonly held definition refers to the use of interchangeable modules to alter the performance or abilities of a piece of equipment. This version of modularity has become popularized most prominently by the 50-dton modular cutter.

Modularity can also refer to a method of construction, where individual pieces of an item of equipment or a vessel are assembled separately, then combined to create the final product.

These two techniques can be referred to as *modular operations* and *modular construction*, respectively.

MODULAR OPERATIONS

Modular operations can be found in many venues of Imperial industry, but nowhere more prominently than in space vessels. The term covers those vessels that possess standardized subcomponents ("modules") which can be quickly and easily replaced with modules of different function.

There are basically two different forms of modular vessel. The most rare kind is the fully modular vessel, a craft where any part of the ship can be swapped out and exchanged. The more common method is a "normal" craft that devotes a portion of its displacement to the use of modules. The modular cutter falls into the latter category.

MODULAR VESSELS

In a purely modular vessel, every section of the ship is a separate module. The craft can be assembled on the fly like a puzzle: Select a control module, the appropriate payload module(s), and a drive module. Put them all together, and you have a ship. Want to go faster? Swap your drive module for a larger one. Need more cargo? Add more cargo modules.

Terminology

Some confusion can result from the many usages of the words "module" and "modular."

GURPS Traveller has a modular ship construction system, which is designed to make it easy for players to create ships, but does not imply the ships would be modularly built.

In order to avoid confusion, this book refers to modules from the construction system as *components* or (when clarity would not be compromised) *component modules*, while any true modules built with the system will be called *modules* if streamlined, *pallets* if unstreamlined.

While not entirely consistent with previous *GURPS Traveller* books, it should reduce confusion in this book, where modules are frequently discussed on several different levels.

Modular Vessels and Other Races

The usage of modular technologies varies across known space.

Aslan Hierate

The Aslan, as a rule, do not use modular technologies. Modular vessels are not considered artistic or stylish enough to warrant their inclusion in fleet actions. A handful of civilian exceptions may exist, but the majority of clans do not posses any modular craft.

Droyne

Modern Droyne are not known to use modular techniques or vessels, except when purchased from the Imperium directly. Ancient vessels were often fully modular (see p. 7), and able to reconfigure themselves at a moment's notice. Like all things Ancient, ship designs varied from world to world.

Hive Federation

Of all the races, only the Hivers use modular craft more than the Imperium. Hivers use a 25-dton module as their standard, rather than the Imperial 30-dton variety. This has the effect of allowing Hiver modules to be used in Imperial craft (with some effort) while Imperial modules cannot easily be used in Hiver vessels. The Hiver see no problem with this – it allows their modules to be exported to the Imperium while preventing many modules from being imported. LSP and other Imperial corporations have issued some complaints, but no action has been taken yet, not the least because there isn't any obvious agency in the Federation to act upon their complaints.

Solomani Confederation

The Solomani have been known to use modular-construction techniques, and have several vessels similar to the modular cutter. For the most part, modules are interchangeable with Imperial cutters with a little effort (approximately 30 minutes' work with a mechanical tool set).

Continued on next page . . .

Truly modular vessels are rare, however, due to the complex construction issues involved. The primary concern is data and power transmission; how does information and energy get shared among all of the individual pieces of the design? Each module must be able to deal with any combination of companion modules, and great care must be taken to ensure that every module gets the proper amount of energy and the correct control and data configuration.

MODULE-USING VESSELS

A more common method of using modules is to have a vessel that is for the most part complete even without the modules. The modules become a form of payload that enhances or adds to the performance or abilities of the parent craft. The modular cutter falls into this category: The primary hull possesses controls, life support, power plant, control surfaces, and drives. It can operate without any module installed (even if it suffers limited acceleration). However, the cutter can be redefined simply by inserting the proper module into its central hull.

METHODS OF MODULE USE

Spacecraft can use modules in a variety of ways, even if they were not specifically designed for module use, and many conventionally-designed ships have been retrofitted to carry modules.

CARGO BAYS/SPACEDOCKS

The most obvious way a ship can utilize a module, even if not specifically constructed for it, is to place the module in a cargo bay or spacedock. Most bays have power connectors, data ports, and tie-down points so that the module can be integrated into the ship's systems, assuming standard connectors.

Obviously, an internal bay is not the best way to utilize a module. The first problem is space; in order to be useful, the module cannot simply be stacked like cargo. It must be placed in a specific fashion. Modules placed in cargo bays normally take twice as much space as they displace – a cutter module in a cargo bay takes up 60 displacement tons, not 30. This assumes that the module is going to be used while in the bay. If the module is simply being transported, it can be treated like normal cargo and stored at its normal displacement.

Modules stored in spacedocks are treated like vessels; the spacedock must be at least twice as large as the module. In any case, the space where the module is stored must possess the proper dimensions for what are often odd-sized units; a cutter module is 14 yards long and 7 yards high, too tall for the cargo decks of many small merchants.

The second problem is that the module has no access to the exterior of the parent ship. This may be completely irrelevant, in the case of passenger or quarters modules, for example. However, it makes no sense to place a weapon or sensor module in a cargo bay unless you are merely transporting it.

Installing modules in cargo bays and docks costs nothing, and takes the same amount of time to stow as normal cargo would take.

VEHICLE BAYS

Another method of storing a module is a vehicle bay. Unlike a cargo bay or spacedock, a vehicle bay is a highly efficient way of storing a module, requiring only one additional space for every 20 spaces of module (thus, a cutter-module vehicle bay takes 32 spaces). However, a vehicle bay must be specifically designed for the item that it carries – a 30-ton vehicle bay for a ship's boat will not carry a cutter module, and vice-versa.

Vehicle bays do allow limited access by the module to the exterior of the parent craft. If the bay is designed properly, it can be assumed that 50% (round up) of the module's weapons, hatches, sensors, and other exterior features can be properly utilized.

On vessels carrying several modules for subordinate craft (such as the *Broadsword*-class mercenary cruiser), modules are often stored in internal vehicle bays. Internal vehicle bays are storage slots that do not have access to the exterior of the carrying vessel – instead, they have access to a larger vehicle bay or spacedock where the subordinate craft is stored. Often, the internal bay mounts powered rails, cranes, or arms for the manipulation of the module and ease of attachment and detachment.

EXTERNAL LASHINGS

The most expedient, but least reliable, method of attaching a module is to simply lash it to the parent hull, using tie-downs, quick-welds, or other simple methods. It costs about Cr100 in materials to lash a cutter module to a hull.

However, lashing is the least useful of the methods, as it allows for no interaction between the module and the parent vessel. While power and data cords can be strung between the module and parent, such jury-rigging rarely works as reliably as dedicated channels, and it is prone to break down if the ship suffers any sort of external damage.

The tie-downs or weld-points also are extremely vulnerable to damage. If the carried module takes damage in combat, the connectors must make a HT roll at -1 for every 500 points of damage before DR is applied. A tie-down usually has HT 10; welds can have HT 5-12 depending on the welder's skill roll.

A failed roll means the module breaks free, doing 2d×10 damage that bypasses any armor to the frames of both module and host vessel. A critical failure means the breakaway module *rams* the parent ship; consult the major-damage table on p. GT174.

Ships that use lashing also must accelerate modestly. Each time the ship exceeds 2 Gs, make a HT+5 roll at -1 per 0.2 Gs over 2 Gs. Roll once per hour for extended periods of high acceleration. The results are the same as those for breakaways resulting from combat damage.

Modular Vessels and Other Races

[Continued]

Two Thousand Worlds

The K'kree have never been known to use modular technology. Due to their resistance to change, it is considered unlikely that they will ever have modular craft. Any such modular craft, of course, would be large – K'kree have no cutter-sized vessels outside of the military.

Vargr

Like all things Vargr, modular use varies from world to world, sector to sector. Some areas of the Extents are known to use modular craft often – both Imperial imports and locally constructed versions. Other areas shun modular designs completely. Modular vessels are more common along the Imperial border, where Vargr designers are influenced by Imperial craft. Vargr modular quality varies greatly as well, ranging from high-quality, useful craft to barely functional vessels that break apart when under any sort of stress.

Zhodani Consulate

Although they are a practical people, the Zhodani Consulate has not embraced modular vessels in the same fashion as their Imperial neighbors. There is no doubt that they have the skill and technology to develop such craft, but the Consulate has chosen to concentrate on more specialized vessels. Experts point to the slightly lagging tech level of the Consulate as the reason – TL11 Consulate vessels need to excel at their assigned tasks if they wish to face off with an equivalent TL12 Imperial vessel. Modular craft would be seen as wasteful in such situations.

Different Brands, Different Cutters

The designs contained within this book are the standard versions, normally produced by Ling Standard Products or a licensed subsidiary. But the cutter design has been out for quite a long time, and other companies manufacture their own products in the same niche, many of which are simple variations (or outright copies) of the LSP standard.

For truly unique vessels, a new design should be created using the rules in **GURPS Traveller**. However, for simple variations of the standard cutter and modules, GMs should feel free to tweak the existing designs to provide variety. Examples might include:

General Products MD-893: A high-quality design based on the standard TL10 cutter, the MD-893 was the cutter of choice of the Imperial Navy until the newer TL12 version came along. It is considered to be one of the most robust and well-designed cutters, able to take a lot of abuse and punishment. Changes: +200 HP for cutter. Cost +MCr0.2.

Kelso Starworks Moducraft: At the lower end of the spectrum, the KS Moducraft is a craft that has been through many revisions, all of them to correct design flaws and Imperial-regulation violations. The design suffers from a number of structural problems, and many of the standard modules cannot be safely carried. However, its low cost has created a booming market, particularly with free traders and merchantmen interested in the highest profit margin. Changes: Maximum load 150 tons, HT -1. Cost -MCr0.6.

Remember that a really serious flaw will make a design unworkable, and a potential deathtrap for players. This makes for an interesting adventure, but the GM's background must explain why a design with known flaws is in service . . . or why the party is the first to encounter those flaws.

MODULAR COUPLINGS

Modular couplings are often used for module stowage. A modular coupling is a dedicated attachment point on a hull, designed to mate to a specific attachment point on another hull. Unlike grapples and cradles, couplings are not generic – a 30-ton cutter-module coupling will not hold a 30-ton ship's boat. They are superior to grapples in that they do not require any interior space. However, they are not as strong as grapples can be, nor do they have the versatility of grapples. See p. 20 for details.

INTRINSIC COUPLINGS

Intrinsic couplings are modular couplings around which the host vessel's hull has been designed; the 50-dton modular cutter uses this technique. They greatly increase the amount of mass that a modular coupling can safely handle, but present unique drawbacks of their own. See p. 21 for details.

EXTERNAL GRAPPLES

While external and intrinsic couplings are useful, they are limited by the fact that they can attach to only one type of module or small craft. Grapples (also called cradles) are larger, more complex connective devices that can connect to any object (or objects) that do not exceed the load rating of the grapple. Grapples have no real limitations in their operations, although they are limited by the surface area of the parent ship and are rather heavy.

MODULE USE

The proper use of modules is an elaborate affair designed to improve efficiency. Module use by itself is rarely more profitable than dedicated vessels, so the day-to-day operation of modules needs to be as smooth as possible.

MAINTENANCE

Modules in regular usage require maintenance. Modules mounted in a vehicle bay, internal vehicle bay, or external to the parent craft cannot be easily maintained, so the ability to remove the module for proper maintenance must be factored into operations.

ATTACHMENT OPERATIONS

By their very nature, modular attachment and detachment operations are designed to be quick and simple. In theory, attaching a module requires only that the unit be slid into place, the clamps locked, and connections made.

Of course, modules are often extremely heavy and large, and thus require equipment to properly move. On the ground, lifters, forklifts, cranes, and exoskeleton loaders can all be used to install a module. In null gravity, no tools are needed (even a single person can slowly shove a massive module) but great care must be taken – the inertia of a module can be a difficult thing to stop. Module-attachment accidents, while not common, are certainly not unheard of. The most common problem is the "runaway module," a module moved by an inexperienced loader that gains too much momentum and smashes into the parent craft or crushes equipment or personnel. Most starports require their cutter loaders to possess certification for heavy loading and equipment operation.

Under normal conditions, GMs can assume that a module can be attached without incident. The following table gives examples of the time required to attach a 30-ton cutter module to various connectors. Other modules would possess similar handling times, adjusted by their size.

Attachment Type	Time to Attach	Skill Mod.
Cargo	30 minutes	-2
Spacedock	20 minutes	-1
Vehicle Bay	10 minutes	0
External Lashing	20 minutes	-3
Modular/Intrinsic Coupling	5 minutes	0
External Grapple	10 minutes	-1

The above assumes non-combat, non-hurried, and safe conditions. In other situations, a skill roll vs. Freight Handling (often modified by Free Fall) should be made to determine if a mishap occurs, with the penalties listed in the table.

Should a mishap occur, the GM should determine the effects. Possibilities include damage to the module, damage to the parent craft, injury, or attachment failure. Attachment failure is particularly dangerous if unnoticed – as soon as any stress is applied to the module and connection points, the module will violently detach, possibly doing a great deal of damage; see the rules for breakaway modules under *External Lashings*, p. 9.

DETACHMENT OPERATIONS

In general, detaching a module takes less time than attaching one. The following table shows the times necessary to detach a 30-ton cutter module safely.

Attachment Type	Time to Detach
Cargo	10 minutes
Spacedock	10 minutes
Vehicle Bay	5 minutes
External Lashing	10 minutes
Modular/Intrinsic Coupling	2 minutes
External Grapple	5 minutes

If caution is thrown to the wind, the times listed above can be halved. A Freight Handling roll is required at -2 for every minute saved. Failed rolls require that the full time be taken, or more, with damage to the module, parent ship, or handlers on critical failures.

Modular Craft in Combat

The addition of modular components affects combat in two ways – hit resolution and damage.

Usually, modules that are stowed in a cargo hold, spacedock, or vehicle bay only take damage when the host vessel is attacked and the appropriate damage results are achieved. Otherwise, modules are treated as distinct vessels, targeted separately from the host vessel with their own size modifier. (Alternately, the rules on p. VE177 can be used to randomly assign hit location to a targeted module-carrying vessel. The module should be substituted for one of the subassemblies listed in the table there, using its size relative to the host vessel as a guideline, before rolling for hit location.)

Other than external lashings (see p. 9), modules rarely break away in combat. In all cases other than external lashings, whenever an individually targeted module or its host vessel must roll on the major-damage table on p. GT174 as a result of taking fire in combat, substitute a breakaway module for the normal results of rolling a 12.

The PLANKWELL-CLASS Battleship

The primary example of the success of modular construction is the *Plankwell*-class battleship. This 200,000-dton combat vessel served with honor in the Fifth Frontier War, earning an impressive combat record.

The ship is constructed around a drive section and keel, with modular sections attached around the keel. While there was concern about the vulnerability of the attachment points, the *Plankwell's* actual performance dismissed such fears. The admiralty currently has several more hulls under construction at Depot/Deneb.

"You keep seeing the reports concerning the **Plankwell** *and how the modular design is just as strong as any other? Well, don't believe anything you hear. Sure, maybe those failures were caused by something other than structural problems, but I do know that the acceleration curves of that beast are a bit skewed due to the vulnerability of the weld points. I wouldn't want to serve on one, that's for sure."*
    – unnamed naval rating,
    Depot/Deneb

The Radiant Princess Disaster

The most widely known example of a modular-construction failure was the destruction of the 100,000-dton passenger liner *Radiant Princess*. The luxurious vessel was constructed as four separate components (drives, power, passengers, and operations) at five separate construction sites (the drives section was transferred to another location for jump-unit construction). The vessel performed adequately during trials, and was certified flight ready. On her maiden voyage, she carried over 11,000 people, including the Baron von Teilk and his retinue. Unfortunately, a power-coupling mismatch had occurred during the assembly of the drives and power sections. The problem did not surface during trials, but on the first voyage the fusion plant had to deal with the power demands of the huge passenger complement. Upon energizing the jump grid, a conduit overloaded and surged, causing disruption in both the jump machinery and the power-distribution system. In a spectacular display of pyrotechnics, the *Radiant Princess* exploded and misjumped simultaneously. TAS news crews and Moran flight control observed the explosion, and knew a catastrophic failure had occurred.

The wreckage appeared nine days later on the fringes of the Mora system, with all hands lost. The incident is still under investigation, and charges are expected against several of the construction yards.

*"I remember when the **Princess** died; I was watching on the 3V. You could see the jump grid firing; the light blue traces sparkling against the blackness of space. It was a beautiful sight – this huge, yet graceful ship all lit up for its launching, hull lights sparkling. Then you saw the first sign of trouble – actual arcs of blue energy dancing along the hull, jumping from gridline to gridline. As she began to jump, and the image drew into itself, there was a brilliant flash of light as the stern end of the ship blew apart in a colorful explosion that just faded into jumpspace. It seems horrible to say, but it was actually beautiful. But we knew that they were doomed – so it was a tragic beauty."*
– Luris Hafurn,
TAS Correspondent

In certain operations, explosive bolts are mounted on the module locks to rapidly separate the module and parent craft. When activated, the bolts will destroy any clamps or connectors, while a chemical thruster will shove the module away from the parent craft. When explosive separation is use, the pilot of the cutter must make a Piloting roll; on a critical miss, damage is done per the major-damage table on p. GT174.

Explosive separation should not be used on the ground – severe damage to the module, parent vessel, and nearby personnel almost certainly will occur.

STANDALONE OPERATIONS

In addition to being used to augment the abilities of a parent vessel, modules are often used by themselves. Many modules can serve as stations, either in space or dirtside. In frontier areas in particular, modular stations are not uncommon. Collections of modules are connected by passageways or frames making large habitats.

In order to be used independently, modules must possess the necessary engineering and life-support components – they obviously cannot draw power or supplies from a parent vessel. When connected together to form a larger structure, care must be taken that all of the power and material needs of all the modules are met.

Connecting or disconnecting two modules takes the same amount of time as normal module attachments and detachments.

MODULAR CONSTRUCTION

The Imperium's other modular technology, modular construction, also has strong applications in the construction of small craft and starships.

Modular construction is the process of building a piece of equipment or a vessel in discrete pieces, and then assembling the pieces to create the final product. While nearly every vessel constructed uses this method in some form, a true modular-construction project is one where significant portions of the overall structure are constructed separately, and then assembled into the final work.

It should be noted that modular construction and modular operations are not mutually exclusive – indeed, vessels that use modules are often constructed using modular techniques.

Modular construction is often touted for its efficiency, as individual factories or construction centers can focus on building a single component (or a small set), thus improving output through familiarity. Such a system relies on the old business adage, "We do one thing, but we do it well," allowing specialization to be an acceptable business model. Modular construction also encourages subcontracting – one company builds the drives, another the quarters, and yet another the weapons. Modular construction can also improve maintenance – if a particular section is failing, the entire section can be removed and replaced, often an easier and faster process than trying to repair or replace a non-modular component.

Opponents of the modular-construction technique cite structural weakness and mismatched modules as their reasons for discounting the method. If designed improperly, a vessel built using modular construction may suffer from structural weak points, particularly at the junctions where modules are connected. Even though ships constructed in this fashion are not explicitly designed to separate, operational stress (particularly combat) can cause sections to be ripped away, causing massive damage. It is particularly a concern for military craft, which is why the Navy has been hesitant to use the technique.

A more serious problem occurs when separate module contractors produce sections that are not 100% compatible. Miscommunication or construction errors can cause connectors to mismatch, power systems to be insufficient, data protocols to be incompatible, and an array of other problems. Such errors would be caught during the basic construction of a non-modular craft, and steps would be taken to correct the problem. But with modular construction, each section is normally completely finished before being brought together for final assembly. At that point of construction, mismatched components can be costly and time-consuming to repair. The worst case is when the sections *almost* match, and are connected, but the small difference in power, data, or structural connection causes some sort of failure, often catastrophic.

Interestingly, detailed studies have failed to prove one technique more financially sound than the other. While modular construction is often more efficient, and efficiency can translate directly into financial savings, it also has to deal with transport costs and the additional costs of final assembly – particularly if there are assembly problems.

Modular construction is primarily used in the commercial-freight sector. Efficiency directly corresponds to financial gain, tolerances can be less stringent since performance is rarely a top priority, and personnel safety is dealt with more easily since most freight craft carry no passengers. Other vessels are normally constructed using normal, non-modular techniques.

"You think cutters don't have problems? You obviously didn't hear about that snafu they had at Alell. The contractor for the new Grande Highport was trying to save a few credits, so she bought a slew of KS Moducrafts for cargo movers and construction tugs. Problem was, she didn't share that information with the dockloaders, who packed the cargo modules solid with superdense metal for the station frame. Five minutes into the flight, they hit some turbulence and the frame buckled. Those beams fell and tore up the construction below. Miracle they didn't kill anybody.

"I hear they got a new contractor now."

*– Markus Dereus,
construction worker, Alell*

"You think any old ship jockey can handle this beast? You're talking 50 displacement tons of temperamental craft. You gotta worry about clamp faults, the structural strength of the spine, and the fact that your center of gravity and performance parameters can change as quick as a module swap. Not to mention tryin' to steer this thing without a module. If you don't have a good pilot, all you're gonna have is a broken cutter with a snapped spine . . ."
– Denil Errando, SPA Cutter Pilot

DISCOURAGED DISADVANTAGES

The regulatory demands placed upon commercial and military pilots make it unlikely that they will suffer from certain disadvantages. Should a PC possess any of these disadvantages, the player will need to explain why his character hasn't had his cutter license and flight privileges revoked:

Addiction (to an illegal substance), Alcoholism, Amnesia, Bad Back, Blindness, Cannot Learn, Color Blindness, Confused, Deafness, Delusions, Dependency, Dwarfism, Dyslexia, Epilepsy, Flashbacks, Gigantism, Hunchback, Lame, Mute, Night Blindness, No Depth Perception, One Arm, One Eye, One Hand, Quadriplegic, Terminally Ill.

FLIGHT CERTIFICATION

Per the certification rules in *GURPS Traveller Far Trader*, pp. 82-85, flight certification is a 0-point advantage that gives a pilot the legal right to operate a given type of vessel. Any character with Piloting (Spaceship)-12 and Astrogation-12 can obtain flight certification for the cutter, which is usually required for employment as a cutter pilot. The best-paying jobs usually will require the more rigorous limited mate's license, p. T:FT83.

CHARACTER TEMPLATES

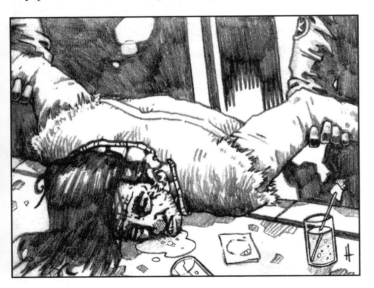

Since their job is both pervasive in Imperial space operations and unique, cutter pilots tend to develop their own specialized skill sets.

MARINE CUTTER PILOT

95 POINTS

In the Imperial Marines, assault cutters are usually crewed by senior NCOs who have received training through the Naval Flight School. The Marines prefer their own pilots over Navy loaners, particularly in combat operations. It is worth noting that not only are these individuals pilots, they are Marines. Each is fully trained in using battledress, energy weapons, and all of the other skills that make the Marines such a fearsome fighting force. See *GURPS Traveller Ground Forces* for more detail on Marine characters.

Attributes: ST 11 [10]; DX 12 [20]; IQ 12 [20]; HT 11 [10].

Advantages: Fit [5]; G-Experience [10]; Military Rank 1 [5]; Panimmunity [5]. Plus 10 additional points in Acceleration Tolerance [10]; Alertness [5/level]; Cool [1]; Combat Reflexes [15]; Danger Sense [15]; Extra Fatigue 1-4 [3/level]; Extra Hit Points 1-4 [5/level]; Fearlessness [2/level]; G-Experience [10]; Hard to Kill 1-2 [5/level]; High Pain Threshold [10]; Improved G-Tolerance [5/level]; Less Sleep 1-5 [3/level]; Night Vision [10]; Peripheral Vision [15]; Strong Will [4/level]; Toughness [10 or 25]; or *one* of Collected [5], Composed [5], or Imperturbable [10].

Disadvantages: Duty (Imperial Marines, 15 or less) [-15] and -20 points from Bloodlust [-10]; Callous [-6]; Chummy [-5]; Code of Honor (Enlisted Man's) [-10]; Compulsive Behavior (any) [-5 to -15]; Dependents [Varies]; Fanaticism (Patriotism) [-15]; Gluttony [-5]; Greed [-15]; Intolerance [Varies]; Laziness [-10]; Lecherousness [-15]; Obsession (Complete any mission, no matter how dangerous) [-5 to

-15]; Odious Personal Habits [-5 to -15]; Overconfidence [-10]; Post-Combat Shakes [-5]; and Stubbornness [-5].

Primary Skills: Armoury (Battlesuit) (M/A) IQ-1 [1]-11; Astrogation (M/A) IQ [2]-12; Battlesuit (P/A) DX [2]-12; Beam Weapon (Fusion) (P/E) DX+2 [1]-14*; Demolition (M/A) IQ [2]-12; Electronics Operation (Comm) (M/A) IQ-1 [1]-11; Electronics Operation (Sensors) (M/A) IQ-1 [1]-11; First Aid (M/E) IQ-1 [1/2]-11; Freight Handling (M/A) IQ-1 [1]-11; Gunner (Guided missile) (P/A) DX [1/2]-12*; Guns (Light auto) (P/E) DX+2 [1]-14*; Free Fall (P/A) DX [2]-12; NBC Warfare (M/A) IQ-1 [1]-11; Parachuting (P/E) DX [1]-12; Piloting (Grav) (P/A) DX-1 [1]-11 (Spaceship) (P/A) DX [2]-12; Savoir-Faire (Military) (M/E) IQ-1 [1/2]-11; Shortsword (P/A) DX-2 [1/2]-10; Survival (type) (M/A) IQ-1 [1]-11; Tactics (M/H) IQ-1 [2]-11; Throwing (P/H) DX-1 [2]-11.

Secondary Skills: Administration (M/A) IQ-1 [1]-11; Area Knowledge (Naval base or large warship) (M/E) IQ [1]-12; Brawling (P/E) DX [1]-12; Gunner (Beam) (P/A) DX+1 [1]-13*; Knife (P/E) DX [1]-12; Leadership (M/A) IQ [2]-12; Scrounging (M/E) IQ [1]-12; Traps (M/A) IQ-1 [1]-11.

*Includes +2 for IQ

NAVY CUTTER PILOT 90 POINTS

As in the Imperial Marines, most naval cutter pilots are senior NCOs. However, there is more variation in the Navy, and it is not unknown for a junior rating to be assigned to pilot a "taxi," or an officer to be given command of a cutter outfitted for an important in-system task such as sensor-picket, escort, or ECM duties.

The following template assumes the standard senior NCO cutter pilot. A junior rating will have less (or no) Military Rank, and little or no Administration, Leadership, and Tactics. An officer will have higher Military Rank, and perhaps more (or higher) skills.

Attributes: ST 10 [0], DX 12 [20], IQ 12 [20], HT 11 [10].

Advantages: G-Experience [10]; Military Rank 1 [5]; and a total of 15 points in 3D Spatial Sense [10], Acceleration Tolerance [10], Combat Reflexes [15], Fit [5], Improved G-Tolerance [10], and Reputation (Decorated) [Varies].

Disadvantages: Duty (Imperial Navy, 15 or less) [-15] and a total of -10 points chosen from Chummy or Gregarious [-5 or -10]; Code of Honor (Soldier's) [-5]; Fanaticism (Patriotism) [-15]; Intolerance (Enemy race or culture, Pirates, etc.) [-5]; Overconfidence or Glory Hound [-10 or -15]; and Sense of Duty (Comrades in arms) [-5].

Primary Skills: Administration (M/A) IQ-1 [1]-11; Area Knowledge (System or sector) (M/E) IQ+1 [2]-13; Astrogation (M/A) IQ+1 [4]-13; Free Fall (P/A) DX+1 [4]-13; Leadership (M/A) IQ [2]-12; Piloting (Spaceship) (P/A) DX+2 [8]-14; Savoir-Faire (Military) (M/E) IQ+1 [2]-13; Tactics (Space) (M/H) IQ-1 [2]-11; and Vacc Suit (M/A) IQ+1 [4]-13.

Secondary Skills: Computer Operation (M/E) IQ [1]-12; Shortsword (P/A) DX [2]-12; and either Beam Weapons (any) or Guns (any), both (P/E) DX+2 [1]-14*.

Background Skills: A total of 2 points in any of Scrounging (M/E); Administration or Heraldry (Ship's Markings), both (M/A); Brawling (P/E); or Carousing (P/A) HT.

*Includes +2 for IQ

SCOUT CUTTER PILOT 60 POINTS

The IISS has a true love of the versatile modular cutter, and its cutter pilots are considered some of the best around. While a Marine or naval pilot might have to deal with combat situations, a scout has to be able to tackle foreign environments and weather, strange natural phenomena, covert flights, and the occasional combat situation. Most Scout pilots become attached to their assigned vehicle, and hull decorations much like military nose art are not uncommon. See *GURPS Traveller First In* for more information on Scouts.

Attributes: ST 10 [0]; DX 11 [10]; IQ 12 [20]; HT 11 [10].

Advantages: A total of 15 points chosen from Administrative Rank 1-5 [5/level]; Common Sense [10]; Fit [5]; Intuition [15]; Luck [15]; Mathematical Ability [10]; Sanctity [5]; Single-Minded [5]; Strong Will [4/level]; and Versatile [5].

Disadvantages: Duty (Scout Service, 15 or less) [-15] and a total of -15 points chosen from Code of Honor (Scouts) [-5]; Curious [-5 to -15]; Honesty [-10]; Impulsiveness [-10]; Overconfidence [-10]; Poverty (Struggling) [-10]; Primitive [-5/level]; Shyness [-5 to -15]; Truthfulness [-5]; Uneducated [-5]; Workaholic [-5]; and Xenophilia [-5 or -15].

Primary Skills: Astrogation (M/A) IQ [2]-12; Freight Handling (M/A) IQ-1 [1]-11; Mechanic (any) (M/A) IQ+2 [6]-14; Piloting (Spaceship) (P/A) DX+2 [8]-13; and *one* of Computer Operation (M/E) IQ+2 [4]-14 *or* Electronics Operation (any) (M/A) IQ+1 [4]-13.

Secondary Skills: Administration (M/A) IQ [2]-12; Free Fall (P/A) DX+1 [4]-12; Scrounging (M/E) IQ [1]-12; and Vacc Suit (M/A) IQ [2]-12.

Background Skills: A total of 5 points in Electronics (any) or Engineer (any), both (M/H); Armoury (any), Electronics Operation (any), Mechanic (any), Shipbuilding (Starship), Streetwise, or Survival (any), all (M/A); Driving (any) or Piloting (Contragravity), both (P/A); or Beam Weapons (any) or Guns (any), both (P/E).

Customization Notes: At least some leftover points should be spent on skills from the character's home-planet background. Someone from an agricultural world might have Agronomy, low-tech Craft skills, or extra Survival. Someone from a more urbanized environment might have extra Social or Thief/Spy skills.

SPA CUTTER PILOT 65 POINTS

Starport Authority cutter pilots are normally recruited from local pilots that are familiar with weather patterns and local flight regulations. They can be found operating cargo flights and passenger transfers.

Attributes: ST 10 [0]; DX 11 [10]; IQ 12 [20]; HT 10 [10].

Advantages: A total of 20 points chosen from Administrative Rank 1-5 [5/level]; Common Sense [10]; Fit [5]; Jack-of-All-Trades [10/level]; Mathematical Ability [10]; Sanctity [5]; Single-Minded [5]; and Versatile [5].

Disadvantages: A total of -15 points chosen from Curious [-5 to -15]; Honesty [-10]; Overconfidence [-10]; Primitive [-5/level]; Truthfulness [-5]; Uneducated [-5]; and Workaholic [-5].

Primary Skills: Area Knowledge (Starport) (M/E) IQ+1 [2]-13; Astrogation (M/A) IQ [2]-12; Freight Handling (M/A) IQ [2]-12; Mechanic (any) (M/A) IQ+2 [6]-14; Piloting (Spaceship) (P/A) DX+1 [4]-12; and *one* of Computer Operation (M/E) IQ+2 [4]-14, Electronics Operation (any) (M/A) IQ+1 [4]-13, Electronics (M/H) IQ [4]-12, *or* Engineer (any) (M/H) IQ [4]-12.

Secondary Skills: Administration (M/A) IQ+1 [4]-13 and Scrounging (M/E) IQ [1]-12.

Background Skills: A total of 5 points in Electronics (any) or Engineer (any), both (M/H); Armoury (any), Electronics Operation (any), Mechanic (any), all (M/A); and Driving (any) or Piloting (Contragravity), both (P/A).

CHAPTER FOUR

Vessels, Vehicles, and Equipment

The modular cutter's popularity has spawned a great deal of support equipment, from specialized cutters and modules to a variety of mounting gear. Very few operations will incorporate all of the equipment listed in this chapter, but many Imperial services and corporations will have a large deal of it in inventory.

NEW EQUIPMENT

The following equipment is primarily marketed to support operations with the 30-dton module, though some of it applies to bringing other equipment in spec with 30-dton modular operations.

CONNECTORS

Several cutter modules are designed to operate separately from any parent vessel, serving as bases, laboratories, or stations. While some of these modules can operate alone, often they are combined with other modules to create larger, more useful facilities. The use of modules in this fashion has become common enough that several modules have been designed *solely* for use in stations and facilities.

Modules do not have clamps or mounting points themselves. Thus, an external method of attaching units must be provided. Three solutions are generally available.

Ring Couplings

Ring couplings provide direct end-to-end connection between two 30-dton modules. A module can be connected to two other modules, by placing ring connectors on each end. Modules can be moved like a "space train" using ring couplers, but each coupler is only rated for 60 standard tons. This can usually be ignored when no acceleration stress is to take place (such as at an orbiting space station made of modules), but is a limiting factor for transport operations. Most modules will be too heavy to move in this fashion, at least when loaded with cargo.

Hard Locks

For orbital assemblies, hard locks can act as a central hub for two to six modules. The hard locks provide the couplings to connect up to the listed number of modules, as well as the necessary airlocks, power connectors, and datalinks between the various components. They do not suffer the mass restrictions of ring couplings, above.

Flexible Locks

On planetary surfaces, modules are not usually directly connected. Instead, a flexible, reinforced plastic tube is attached between modules, allowing access between them. Conduits in the tube transfer data, power, and materials among the modules.

Connecting and disconnecting hard locks takes the same amount of time as connecting or disconnecting modules from a cutter; see p. 11. Attaching a flexible connector takes around 15 minutes and requires a mechanical tool set. Disconnecting a flexible connector takes around 30 minutes if properly folded and stowed, but can be done in under 5 minutes if the connector is to be discarded. Ring couplings can be attached or removed in about 10 minutes.

"It has come to my attention that some maintenance crews are disabling the safety interlocks on the flexible locks to speed installation. This can cause the pods to decompress without warning, and is guaranteed to make you unpopular with any survivors."

*– Kristian Wallenburgh, Assistant Chief Engineer, IS **Panthera***

HARD CLAMPS

While very reliable under normal usage, it is not unknown for cutter couplings to malfunction, especially under combat situations; see sidebar, p. 11. In order to prevent such an occurrence while operating under stress, the Imperial Navy developed hard clamps. Hard clamps attach to the cutter and module along the spine and the ends of the module. Unlike the normal coupling, hard clamps are purely mechanical devices that lock into place. Thus, a power surge or combat damage cannot cause the clamps to release prematurely. Installing a complete set of hard clamps takes 15 minutes and requires a mechanical tool set. The module cannot be removed from the cutter until the hard clamps are removed, which must be done manually. Removing the clamps takes around 10 minutes.

HIVER-MODULE SPACER

The Hive Federation also has a modular-cutter design, although it has a cutter and module displacement of 15 and 25 tons rather than 20 and 30 tons. Thus, Imperial modules cannot be mounted on Hiver cutters. To improve the market for Hiver-module use on Imperial cutters, the Federation has marketed a 5-dton "spacer" that attaches to the front end of a Hiver module and allows it to benefit from the increased weight capacity of the intrinsic coupling on an Imperial cutter (see p. 21).

The spacer's purpose is to mate the forward airlock of the Hiver module to the airlock on the Imperial cutter. Only the upper-deck airlock is connected – the lower-deck one is unused when connected to a Hiver module. While a module can be carried without the spacer, it will only be accessible from its rear hatch in such situations.

MODULE LIFTERS

One of the challenges of cutter modules is groundside connection and disconnection, particularly in a frontier situation. Module lifters were designed by the Imperial Marines to facilitate the rapid removal of modules from the assault-cutter frame – an important task to complete quickly when under fire.

Each lifter is a 2'-by-3' box about 6" thick. The upper side features a single magnetic clamp; the underside has a bank of contragravity lifters. Each single lifter can generate 50 stons of lift, adjustable using a small control box connected to the unit. Multiple lifters can be joined to generate more lift if required.

With enough lifters in place, cutter modules can be removed or inserted by battledress- or cargo-lifter-equipped personnel. Users must remember that even though the weight of the module may be reduced or nullified, the mass and inertia of the module is not, so great care must be exercised when handling the modules. A module can be *extremely* difficult to stop once it begins to move.

While initially designed for handling modules, the module lifters can be and often are used for a variety of other tasks.

MODULE STRUT

Normally, when operating without a module, the 50-dton modular cutter is limited to 2 Gs of acceleration to avoid stressing the vessel's structure. The module strut provides the necessary reinforcement to allow a cutter to use its full acceleration without danger of hull failure. The framelike structure clamps into the module space, taking about 5 minutes to install or remove provided the proper tools are available. While the strut does allow higher acceleration, the upper limit on airspeed remains 1,200 mph due to the drag that the open frame creates.

Item	Volume	Mass	Cost
Explosive Bolt Set	44 cf	150 lbs.	KCr23
Flexible Locks			
2 Module	40 cf	400 lbs.	KCr5
3 Module	50 cf	500 lbs.	KCr6
4 Module	60 cf	600 lbs.	KCr7
Hard Clamps	15 cf	40 lbs.	KCr6
Hard Locks			
2 Module	4 dtons	55.7 tons	MCr1.62
3 Module	6 dtons	82.5 tons	MCr2.31
4 Module	8 dtons	109.1 tons	MCr2.98
5 Module	10 dtons	135.5 tons	MCr3.64
6 Module	12 dtons	161.9 tons	MCr4.29
Hiver Module Spacer	5 dtons	7 tons	MCr0.715
Module Lifter (TL12)	3 cf	185 lbs.	KCr10.7
Module Strut	10 dtons	3.65 tons	MCr0.182
Ring Coupling	0.12 dtons	3 tons	KCr12

Several vehicles have been designed specifically to transport cutter modules. Starports often have many of these vehicles to facilitate the storage and groundside operations of modules.

TL6 TRACKED MODULE MOVER

A huge truck, the TMM is capable of transporting a single module weighing no more than 200 standard tons. The flattened body is entirely composed of the module cradle and transmission. A small crew cabin sits on the front left side, providing comfortable seating for two.

Several starports have begun manufacturing a variant with a fusion power plant, but these designs are still quite rare.

The vehicle has a crew of two, the driver and loadmaster, who have computerized duplicate controls, NBC kits, crashwebs, and six man-days of life support. It features a sealed body, four tracks, and a 200-ton external cradle.

Subassemblies: Body +5, 4 Tracks +3 each.
Power & Propulsion: 804-kW standard MHD turbine, 800-kW tracked drivetrain.
Fuel: 1,000-gallon self-sealing tank providing 6.2 hours endurance.
Occupancy: 2 NCS   **Cargo:** 20 cf

Armor	F	RL	B	T	U
Bo:	4/10	4/10	4/10	4/10	4/10

Equipment
Bo: Two 100-mile communicators; 2 GPSs; Complexity 2 small computer with terminal; compact fire-suppression system; one-man airlock [R].

Statistics
Dim.: 10'×10'×22' *Payload:* 200 tons *Lwt.:* 229.8 tons
Volume: 2,240 cf *SizeMod:* +5 *Price:* KCr522

HT: 7 *HP:* 4,500 [Body]   810 [each Track]

gSpeed: 23 *gAccel:* 2 *gDecel:* 20 *gMR:* 0.25 *gSR:* 6
High GP, 8 mph off-road speed.

Design Notes
The 1,400-cf body has an extra-heavy, very cheap frame. It has 66.18 cf of access space and 37.36 cf of empty space. Surface area is 750 sf for the body and 540 sf for the 840 cf of tracks. Armor is cheap metal.

TL10 GRAV MODULE MOVER

A long, flat slab, the GMM is the gravitic counterpart to the TMM. The external cradle is essentially identical, capable of supporting 200 standard tons itself. The crew cabin is mounted in a small section forward and slightly below the cradle unit.

Great care must be used when piloting the GMM, as a massive cutter module, when carried, radically alters the in-flight characteristics of the vehicle. The GMM is a rather unstable craft when under full load, and is best piloted by an experienced individual.

Like the TMM, a fusion-powered variant has begun to appear on the market.

The vehicle has a crew of two, the driver and loadmaster, who have computerized duplicate controls, NBC kits, crashwebs, and six man-days of life support. It features a sealed body and a 200-ton external cradle.

Subassemblies: Body +5.
Power & Propulsion: 2,404-kW standard MHD turbine, 40,000-lb. vectored reactionless thruster, 400,000 lbs. contragravity.
Fuel: 2,000-gallon self-sealing tank providing 5.5 hours endurance.
Occupancy: 2 NCS   **Cargo:** 20 cf

Armor	F	RL	B	T	U
Bo:	4/50	4/50	4/50	4/50	4/50

Equipment
Bo: Two 1,000-mile communicators; navigation instruments; transponder; 2 GPSs; terrain-following radar; 2 Complexity 6 minicomputers with two terminals; compact fire-suppression system; one-man airlock [T].

Statistics
Dim.: 8'×10'×20' *Payload:* 200 tons *Lwt.:* 232.4 tons
Volume: 1,600 cf *SizeMod:* +5 *Price:* KCr566

HT: 7 *HP:* 4,920

aSpeed: 600/261   *aAccel:* 12/2 *aDecel:* 12 *aMR:* 3
aSR: 4
Stall speed 0. Space performance: 0.6 Gs without module/0.1 Gs with.

Design Notes
The body has an extra-heavy, very cheap frame. It has 97.79 cf of access space and 18.35 cf of empty space. Surface area is 820 sf. Armor is cheap metal. Aerial drag is 410 without a module/4,410 with.

TL12 MILITARY MODULE MOVER

Superficially identical to the GMM, the M3 is a TL12 version with slightly more armor and greater lift capacity, capable of lifting the heavier modules used by the advanced, assault, and stealth cutters.

The vehicle has a crew of two, the driver and loadmaster, who have computerized duplicate controls, NBC kits, crashwebs, and six man-days of life support. It features a sealed body and a 390-ton external cradle.

Subassemblies: Body +5.

Power & Propulsion: 5,404-kW fusion plant, 90,000-lb. vectored reactionless thruster, 900,000 lbs. contragravity.

Occupancy: 2 NCS   **Cargo:** 20 cf

Armor

	F	RL	B	T	U
Bo:	4/100	4/100	4/100	4/100	4/100

Equipment

Bo: Two 1,000-mile communicators; navigation instruments; transponder; 2 GPSs; terrain-following radar; 2 Complexity 8 minicomputers with two terminals; compact fire-suppression system; one-man airlock [T].

Statistics

Dim.: 10'×10'×22'   *Payload:* 372.4 tons   *Lwt.:* 422.4 tons
Volume: 2,200 cf   *SizeMod:* +5   *Price:* MCr1.4

HT: 6   *HP:* 6,090

aSpeed: 600/387   *aAccel:* 18/2 *aDecel:* 12   *aMR:* 3
aSR: 4
Stall speed 0. Space performance: 0.9 Gs without module/0.1 Gs with.

Design Notes

The body has an extra-heavy, standard frame. It has 134.016 cf of access space and 31.348 cf of empty space. Surface area is 1,015 sf. Armor is expensive metal. Aerial drag is 507 without a module/4,507 with.

NEW SPACECRAFT/STARSHIP HULLS

The following new hulls have been used for several of the *GURPS Traveller*-based spacecraft and starship designs.

Hull Tonnage	Volume (cf)	Hull Area	TL10 Mass	TL12 Mass	Hull Cost (in MCr)	Size Mod.
25	12,500	3,500	3.5	1.75	0.175/0.42	+7
60	30,000	7,000	7	3.5	0.35/0.84	+7
90	45,000	9,000	9	4.5	0.45/1.08	+8
1,000	500,000	45,000	45	22.5	2.25/5.40	+10

> *"Of course, you know cutters don't need freshers – they just swap out your kidneys with empty ones."*
>
> *– Anton Wilson Peale*

NEW CONSTRUCTION OPTIONS

The following rules and options have been used for several of the vessel designs.

ROBOTIC HULLS

In use by the Hive Federation, robotic hulls allow a vessel to be operated by a robotic brain (not included). Robotic hulls cost twice as much as a normal hull. Note that it is illegal in the Imperium to have purely robotic craft – although robotic hulls are not illegal themselves, they must have living crew on board to operate in Imperial space.

HEAVY AND EXTRA-HEAVY FRAMES

In order to provide a stronger structure to support more weight with couplings, or to increase the hit points of a craft for improved combat performance, ship hulls can be upgraded to heavy or extra-heavy.

Heavy frames double the hull's hit points, but also double its cost and increase its mass by 50%. Extra-heavy frames quadruple the hit points, but multiply hull cost by 5 and mass by 2.

MODULAR COUPLINGS

Modular couplings are linkages commonly used to join a module to a modular craft. These linkages are simple connectors, far less elaborate and expensive than the robotics found in an external grapple. Conversely, modular couplings are not automated – a freight-handler usually must manually perform attachments and detachments. Modular couplings also are dedicated. Only a module of the same "standard" can be attached to a given modular coupling. The most common standard in the Imperium is the "cutter coupling," used by the 30-dton modules for the modular cutter. Coming in a distant second is the "freight coupling" used by the standardized containers described on pp. T:FT56-57.

Modular couplings are designed as hardpoints, per pp. VE94-95. Couplings may be installed on a given hull for up to (0.01 × the ship's hit points) standard tons of module. A coupling weighs 0.05 tons and costs Cr200 per ton of capacity.

Any couplings installed on a small craft take up the space normally available for a turret (but see *Intrinsic Couplings*, p. 21). For ships of 100 displacement tons or greater, each 100 standard tons of modular-coupling capacity takes up the space usually available for one turret.

The standard coupling includes data and power leads. A "dead" coupling can be installed for half the cost of a linked coupling. For double cost, a linked coupling can be *remote-controlled*, allowing the modular-ship operator to detach (but not attach) a module from his crew station. A linked coupling can be made *explosive* (see p. 12) for 5 times normal cost; use this cost in lieu of the add-on explosive-bolt package for other connectors on p. 18.

The modules themselves require no extra cost or weight to fit a given coupling standard.

INTRINSIC COUPLINGS

Standard modular couplings simply tack the module to the hull of a ship, much like a TL7 fighter plane attaches weapons under its wings. An intrinsic coupling makes space for the module within the general outline of the modular ship itself; the module is "inserted" into its coupling like a battery into a radio.

Intrinsic couplings *quadruple* the standard tons of module that a given coupling can carry, because the module is more snugly held by the hull of the modular ship carrying it.

Several factors offset this advantage. First, an intrinsic coupling must be rated for dtons as well as standard tons of capacity. Thus, the standard modular cutter's intrinsic coupling must carry a 30-dton module. Modules of smaller size may be carried, but the coupling will then have only one-quarter its usual weight capacity.

Second, a ship with intrinsic couplings may have restrictions placed on its sAccel rating when it is not carrying modules. The ship's structural integrity is just as dependent on the module as the module's fastening is dependent on the ship's structural integrity. To determine the sAccel limit of a ship with intrinsic couplings, divide the dton capacity of all intrinsic couplings by the displacement of the ship before the couplings are added. Look up the result on the table below:

Dton Ratio	sAccel Limit
0.01 or less	None
0.011-0.5	3
0.51-1	2.5
1.01-1.5	2
1.51-2	1.5
2.01-2.5	1
2.51 or more	0.5

Each time the vessel exceeds its sAccel limit, the pilot should make a Piloting roll at -3, with a further -1 per 0.2 Gs over the limit. Roll once per hour for extended periods of high acceleration. Every failed roll does 6d×50 damage to the vessel's hull, bypassing armor.

Ships with two or more intrinsic couplings will have several sAccel limits, depending on whether all or some modules are missing. Modules that are in place count as host-vessel displacement when comparing empty intrinsic capacity to host-vessel displacement.

Third and finally, in almost all circumstances ships with intrinsic couplings are considered to displace their own hull displacement *plus* the displacement of their intrinsic couplings. Therefore, the 50-dton modular cutter rates as 50 dtons of small

craft when carried by a ship, whether or not it's carrying a module. Standard Imperial practice is to even call the ship by this expanded displacement.

Intrinsic couplings must be added when a ship is designed; they cannot be retrofitted. They do not displace turret capacity as do standard modular couplings.

Example: The 50-dton modular cutter is designed as a 20-ton small craft. This gives it 4,500 hit points. Its maximum intrinsic-coupling capacity in weight is up to (4,500/100×4) or 180 standard tons. We designate that its intrinsic coupling will have the maximum 180 standard tons of capacity with (of course) 30 dtons of volume capacity. The coupling adds 2.25 tons to the cutter's weight and MCr0.009 to its cost. The craft now will be designated as a "50-ton" modular cutter, even though in combat it will be targeted as a 20-ton vessel (the 30-ton module would be targeted separately, unless using the alternate rules on p. 11). Dividing its 30 dtons of module capacity by its 20 dtons of hull size gives a dton ratio of 1.5, which limits sAccel to 2 Gs when a module is not carried. The cutter also takes up space as a 50-dton craft in all circumstances, unless a generous GM allows crafty spacehands to stack cargo carefully around its odd configuration.

NEW COMPONENT MODULES

The following component modules are additions to those presented in the starship-construction rules of *GURPS Traveller*. Some are completely new, while many have previously appeared in *GURPS Traveller* supplements. Some modules in the latter category have minor alterations to their descriptions and statistics. These conform to changes planned for them in the upcoming *GURPS Traveller: Starships*.

Accommodations

These are extended accommodations for craft equipped with bridges but no staterooms. The component module includes full life support for five people, two bunks, associated fusion components, and 9.5 cf of storage for personal gear.

Armoury/Safe

This is a single room with DR 200 reinforced walls and door.

Boarding Clamp

This is an advanced grapple designed to latch onto an enemy ship for boarding purposes. It differs from an ordinary grapple in its reach (slightly longer), its strength (much stronger), and the method in which it attaches to the target vessel. The boarding clamp does significant damage to the hull of the target vessel, whereas normal grapples are designed to attach without damage.

Brig

This is an ordinary stateroom equipped with reinforced walls and door (DR 200), restraints, and a high-security alarm and observation system. It normally holds 1-2 people. Up to 50 could be crammed in for a limited time, but this would overwhelm the two-person life support. A ship or starport with one or two brigs will normally monitor them from the bridge. A larger number of brigs probably will have its own dedicated security station.

Bunkroom

This includes bunks for 16 personnel, with life support, under very cramped conditions. Imperial protocol is to load only four passengers per bunkroom, except for missions of very short duration or emergencies.

Collapsible Tank

This collapsible, self-sealing tank made from light, folding polymers expands into any empty cargo hold or spacedock. Capacity is 400,000 gallons (60,000 cf); it holds 120 dtons (120 standard tons) of jump fuel when full. It can be installed in 0.5-dton increments. A full tank will rupture during maneuvers above 1.5 Gs, spilling its contents.

Communications

There are two different communication components, each detailed below.

Enhanced Communications

These arrays can either provide communications to modules without control components or can augment existing communication systems.

ENHANCED COMMUNICATIONS RANGES
(RATING/RANGE IN MILLIONS OF MILES)

TL	Radio	Maser	Laser	Meson
10	5/5	3/50	2/10	1/1
12	10/5	6/50	6/10	1/2

Xboat Relay

A Scout-base staple, this TL12 component contains a single massive laser communicator with 100 million miles of transmission range and 10 times that in reception. There are three hardened, high-capacity mainframe computers, 5000 terabytes of hardened data storage with double backups, and an energy bank with five hours of operational capacity. The unit is designed for high redundancy, with the three computers checking the other's results and the three sets of data stored in different locations. The laser communicator is used for its very high bandwidth. Even with the usual high level of encryption and error-correction, the unit can upload or download its entire storage capacity in about an hour. The equivalent TL10 component has the same size and cost, but carries only 50 terabytes of data.

Complete Workshop

This provides tools and equipment for up to three individuals using the Armoury, Electronics, Engineering, or Mechanic skills. On large ships, one complete workshop is required for every 60 engineers or mechanics.

Computer System

High-speed, high-complexity computer systems are at the heart of any naval vessel, particularly its fire-control network. This system contains eight high-capacity (+50% to number of programs) computers for use in ships that require more computing resources than the command bridge can provide. Complexity of the computers is equal to TL-2. This system is common in large ships that have a lot of weapons to target and want to be able to run multiple copies of advanced targeting programs.

Drop Capsule Launcher

This is a pair of 700mm missile launchers in a fixed mounting. Rate of fire is 1/10 each, so in one space combat phase the pair can launch 240 capsules. This component can also function as a pair of one-man airlocks.

Drop Capsule Rack

This component module stores up to 16 capsules (with mass of up to 2,000 lbs. each) in ready racks with room for maintenance and loading. The component statistics do not include the mass of the capsules.

Duplicate Control Module

This is a simple cockpit intended to give another piloting position for control of the craft for docking or other delicate maneuvers. It has duplicate controls and a one-person airlock, but no fusion startup, navigation, or independent life-support.

Electronic Warfare Systems

Space combat takes place on more than just the physical plane. Naval vessels must be able to attack and defend themselves from attacks using the electromagnetic spectrum. Electronic warfare suites provide a wide range of offensive and defensive electronic warfare capabilities to naval vessels. At the ranges at which most space battles occur, the effects of these systems are largely ignored. Let one side neglect their preparation in this arena, however, and their opponents will be quick to exploit the error.

Each suite consists of two advanced radar/laser detectors, two area jammers, two blip enhancers, two hardened macroframe computers (Complexity TL-2) with terminals, four radio direction finders, two radio jammers, 24-hour rechargeable power cell, and two crew stations.

The listing for area jammers gives jammer rating/range in miles; the other listings are range in miles. Crew: 2.

ELECTRONIC WARFARE SYSTEMS

TL	Area Jammer Rating/range in miles	RDF Range in miles	Radio Jammer Range in miles
10	7/45	500 million	50,000
12	7/45	5 billion	50,000

Entry

An entry component consists of a passage tube (p. S118) and either a four-person (small) or eight-person (large) airlock.

Evacuation Bay, Basic (TL10)

This contains 12 stretchers and 12 emergency support units, with plenty of access space to move people in and out of them. It also includes 12 man-days of limited life support and a fusion power module. Mostly used by small craft for medevac to a waiting starship.

Evacuation Bay, Advanced (TL10)

This contains 12 automeds and plenty of access space to move people in and out of them. Also includes 12 man-days of limited life support and a fusion power module. Mostly used by small craft for medevac to a waiting starship.

External Cradle

This holds 125 standard tons (250,000 lbs.) of vehicle or module on the outside of the ship's hull. It can be installed in 0.5-dton increments. Vehicles carried this way aren't counted against the ship's internal spaces, but must still be included in jump-drive requirements. They are not protected by the ship's armor. Unlike modular couplings (see p. 10), cradles (also called grapples) are generic in nature, able to attach to any vehicle not exceeding its load rating.

Extra-Heavy Water Cannon

This is a large water projector, suitable for firefighting. It projects 16 gallons per second from a 1,000-gallon tank, each tank holding enough water or fire-extinguisher foam for 125 seconds of use, though connections can be made to a larger external tank. Up to three cannons may be fitted into a standard turret.

Each shot of water puts out a fire in a hex on 1-4 on 1d; a shot of extinguisher foam puts out a fire on 1-5.

Gymnasium

A gym usually contains a wide variety of exercise machines and facilities for both strength and aerobic training. The standard gym can be used by up to four people at a time.

Hull Cutter

A set of articulated fusion cutters, this component allows boarding craft to cut through the armor of enemy ships.

Information Center

A TL12 high-tech military-style operations room for 10-20 people, this component has workstations, a sophisticated array of electronic mapping and display tables (which functions as a fire-direction center), plus several dozen digital cameras for video teleconferencing. The module also includes a hardened Complexity 8 macroframe computer and 10 terminals.

Jammer (TL12)

This component is a smaller version of the Electronic Warfare module. While the general electronic warfare component can extend its protection to other vessels, the jammer unit is designed to cloak the carrying vessel alone. It contains a laser/radar detector, area radar jammer (rating 7, 45-mile range), deceptive radar jammer (rating 7), chaff decoy discharger (40 decoys), infrared jammer (rating 7), and batteries (12 hours' endurance).

Large Room

This also can be called a Hall, Bar, or Conference Room component module. It is a large room, with tables, that can be used as a restaurant, bar, conference room, etc. Each unit can comfortably accommodate 100 people; smaller lounges and conference rooms are included in stateroom volumes. Weight and cost includes furnishings.

Life Support

This component come in two forms – full life support and total life support. Both types come with atmosphere generation, filtering, and reclamation equipment. Water filtration and recovery systems are also included. The total life-support system also includes the ability to create food, usually in the form of plants, yeast-based products, or small animals. The total life-support system can represent hydroponic gardens, small farms, or yeast vats.

System/TL	Capacity
Full Support/10	95
Full Support/11+	500
Total Support/10	25
Total Support/11+	125

MagLev Module

This component provides the machinery necessary to generate 200 standard tons of magnetic lift. The unit includes systems designed to pull power from lift rails as well.

Modular Coupling

This item provides the connectors and the linkages for modular components. As detailed on p. 10, external couplings are designed for specific types of connections, such as "30-dton cutter module." A ship can mount a total of one coupling component for every 100 HP it has. Each component supports 1 standard ton of module.

These components must be "bundled" into larger-capacity couplings upon installation; for instance, a ship with 60,000 hit points could install a single coupling with 600 standard tons of capacity by bundling 600 of these component modules, but then could not use the same coupling to carry 600 1-ton modules or even two 300-ton modules. Refer to the modular-coupling rules on p. 20 for more information.

Morgue

This component includes space for 20 sets of battledress (weighing up to 2,000 lbs. each) and accessories such as flight packs, with room for maintenance and loading. The component statistics do not include the mass of the carried suits.

Office

Each office component holds four offices, with room for three visitors each, or 16 cubicles with no room for visitors. Includes full life support for 16 and space for conference rooms, office-supply storage, etc.

Power Plant

This component provides a fusion core component and fire-suppression system, along with a single one-man airlock. It is intended to be a smaller alternative to the standard Engineering module, much like the Small-Craft Bridge Add-On. Unlike the Small-Craft Bridge Add-On, the power plant offers no accommodations. Three versions are available – a simple power-plant version, a power-plant and gravity version (supplies gravity and 2 Gs of grav compensation to 50 dtons of space), and a power-plant, gravity, and life-support version (identical to the gravity version, also includes full life support for 32 people – but no bunks).

Power Module

This component – when attached to an Engineering, Small Craft Bridge Add-On, or Cockpit Bridge component module – will provide 62.5 megawatts of power.

Probe

This component is designed for the launch and control of long-range probes. The probe component includes three launch systems, a very-long-range laser communicator, a computer terminal, and a roomy crew station. There is storage space for 20 standard IISS probes and 40 modular payload packages for the probes.

Sensor Systems

Sensor suites extend the range and capabilities of shipboard sensors beyond those that come with standard bridge systems. They come in both enhanced and advanced versions.

System/TL	Scan (PESA/AESA/Radscanner)
Enhanced Sensors/10	43/45/37
Enhanced Sensors/11+	45/47/39
Advanced Sensors/10	45/47/38
Advanced Sensors/11+	47/49/40

Small-Craft Bridge Add-On

This unit can be used instead of an Engineering component on craft equipped with a Basic Bridge. It includes fusion-power startup, full life support for five, and a two-man airlock. The TL12 version also includes one bunk.

Stage

A 20'×20' stage area with high ceilings fills this component module. It can be used for dancing, plays, nightclub acts, etc. Includes sophisticated light and sound systems. Normally attached to a Large Room (see p. 24) or Theater (see below) containing the audience.

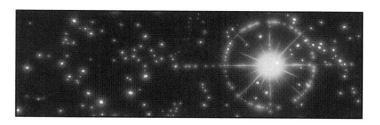

Survey/Traffic Control

This component contains four sets of astronomical instruments, four high-resolution planetary survey arrays, a mainframe computer, eight roomy workstations with computer terminals, and sophisticated holographic-projection devices. It is intended to be used for planetary survey missions or as a flight traffic-control center.

"I've never played one of these pod theaters before . . . say, what do you guys do for entertainment out here when you don't have me around? I don't want to say this place is remote. I mean, it's not really the end of the universe, but you can see it from here.

So anyway, this ham sandwich goes into a Brubek's and orders a brew. Bartender says 'I'm sorry, I can't do that.' Ham sandwich says 'Why not?' Bartender says 'We don't serve food here.'

Hello? Is this an audience or a hologram . . ."

– Anton Wilson Peale,
Live from the Bowman Belt, 001-1119

Swimming Pool

Large passenger liners often have swimming pools. This includes 100 sf of pool (10' deep), 100 sf of deck area, and overhead clearance. Multiple modules can be combined to make larger pools. The finished design should add one Spacedock or Tankage component module per complete Pool component to contain the water in case of loss of gravity.

Tankage

An ultra-light, self-sealing tank, this is suitable for holding most room-temperature and cryogenic liquids. Holds 3,333 gallons.

Theater

This is a small auditorium with 100 roomy seats for the audience, a large holo-projector, and an operator's workstation. Seating is sharply raked to improve the view. It can be used for entertainment or presentations, or as a briefing or situation room. The projector can be stowed, if desired. A stage is not included.

Winch

This can lift 200,000 lbs. in 1 G, or pull up to 400,000 lbs. horizontally at 2 yards per second.

STARSHIP COMPONENT MODULES

System	Space	Mass	Cost (MCr)	Crew
Accommodations	0.5	1	0.008	
Armoury/Safe	1	7	0.03	
Boarding Clamp/10	1	12.1	12	
Boarding Clamp/12	0.5	6.06	6	
Brig/10	4	11.4	0.052	!
Brig/12	4	5.6	0.03	!
Bunkroom/10	4	4.8	0.019	
Bunkroom/12	4	1.92	0.018	
Collapsible Tank	1	10	0.4	
Communications				
Enhanced/10	1.5	18.1	2.1	
Enhanced/12	1.5	16.3	0.67	
Xboat Relay	10.5	126.0	1.390	0-1
Complete Workshop	2.5	15	0.06	
Computer System	1	12	30	
Drop Capsule Launcher	1	12	0.15	
Drop Capsule Racks/10	1	2	0.05	
Drop Capsule Racks/12	1	1.5	0.05	
Duplicate Controls	0.5	0.3	0.003	
Electronic Warfare/10	3	43.7	13	2
Electronic Warfare/12	3	40.4	10.5	2
Enhanced Communications			See *Communications*	
Entry Module, Small	0.5	2	0.007	
Entry Module, Large	1	3	0.011	
Evac. Bay, Basic/10+	2	1.2	0.1	!
Evac. Bay, Adv./10+	4	3.3	0.61	!
External Cradle	1**	12.5**	0.25**	
Extra-Heavy Water Cannon	1	0.31	0.015	1
Gymnasium	2.5	0.5	0.002	
Hull Cutter	0.5	5.4	0.31	
Information Center	4	3	2.8	10-2
Jammer/10	1	14.5	11.3	1
Jammer/12	1	16.5	10.3	1
Large Room	10	0.2	0.003	!
Logistics	5	30	0.12	
Life Support				
Full/10	1	9.6	0.06	
Full/11+	1	5	0.25	
Total/10	1	5	0.03	
Total/11+	1	2.5	0.13	
MagLev	1	4	0.83	
Modular Coupling	0	0.05*	0.001*	
Dead (no linkages)	0	0.05*	0.0005*	
Remote	0	0.05*	0.002*	
Explosive	0	0.05*	0.005*	
Morgue/10	1	2.25	0.07	
Morgue/12	1	1.63	0.07	
Office/10	4	3.62	0.02	!
Office/11+	4	2.16	0.02	!
Power Plant/11+	0.5	1.35	0.156	
with Gravity	0.5	2.37	0.179	
with Gravity and LS	0.5	2.69	0.195	
Power Module/10	1	4	0.4	1/60
Power Module/11	+1	4	0.2	1/100

System	Space	Mass	Cost (MCr)	Crew
Probe	1	1.2	0.033	0-3
Sensors				
Enhanced Sensors/10	4	41.2	27.3	0-1
Enhanced Sensors/11+	4	38.7	26.9	0-1
Advanced Sensors/10	8	82.4	56.8	0-1
Advanced Sensors/11+	8	77.1	56.5	0-1
Small-Craft Bridge Add-On/10	0.5	1.96	0.32	
Small-Craft Bridge Add-On/11+	0.5	1.65	0.15	
Stage	16	0.5	0.004	!
Survey/Traffic Control/10	4	5.31	30.6	4-8
Swimming Pool	6	27/1.5#	0.031	!
Tankage	1	0.16	0.017	
Theater	20	2.1	0.015	!
Winch	1	12.5	0.2*	
Xboat Relay Communications			See *Communications*	

   * Per 1 standard ton carried, maximum number is hull HP/100. Modular couplings count against the mounted-turret limit at a rate of one turret lost per 100 tons of coupling capacity. Intrinsic couplings use the same component module and do not reduce hardpoints; see p. 21. May be installed in fractional increments.

   ** Per 125 standard tons of ship to be carried. External cradles count against the mounted-turret limit at a rate of one turret lost per three cradle components installed.

   # First figure is filled mass, second is empty. Should have one Spacedock or Tankage component per component in highport or starship.

   ! Varies, or GM's discretion.

Extra-Heavy Water Cannon

Malf	Type	Dam	SS	Acc	1/2D	Max
Crit.	Spcl.	4d×4	5	12	200	300

RoF	Weight	Cost	WPS	VPS	CPS
8	610	15,250	12	0.192	0/2*

Cr0 for water, Cr2 for foam.

SMALL CRAFT

The following support vessels can be found across the Imperium engaged in modular operations.

50-TON MODULAR CUTTER (TL10)

The original LSP/CM-50 50-ton modular cutter, designed by LSP, has gone through many changes over the years, and is now manufactured by many different companies. It remains, however, one of the most versatile and useful spaceships in Imperial space.

The standard cutter is a 24-yard-long cylinder 7 yards in diameter. It is broken into three sections: a 4.5-yard-long forward hull, the 14-yard-long module, and a 6-yard-long drive section. The forward hull is a two-level design, with the bridge and primary airlock on the upper level, and electronics, sensors, and a small sleeping area on the lower area. The drive section is almost entirely taken up with the single large thruster unit and the fusion plant that powers it.

The most striking feature of the cutter is the large open area between the forward hull and drive section, where a single 30-dton cutter module can be mounted. A single, long spine connects the forward and drive sections, and provides the coupling points for the module. Each module possesses a slot along its dorsal edge that mates with the spine of the cutter and locks into place. Smaller clamps also secure the ends of the module to the airlocks of the forward hull and drive section.

While the cutter is designed to operate normally with a module locked in place, it is possible to fly without one. The spine connecting the two ends has a narrow access tube that allows movement between the two sections of the main hull. The vessel is not as stable when operating moduleless; safe acceleration is limited to 2 Gs.

The 50-ton modular cutter has a crew of pilot, co-pilot, and engineer. It features a sealed body and a single intrinsic coupling for a 30-dton module weighing up to 180 standard tons.

Subassemblies: SL Hull.
Power & Propulsion: 12 Maneuver.
Occupancy: 5 RCS   **Cargo:** 0.5 dtons

Armor	F	RL	B	T	U
All:	4/100	4/100	4/100	4/100	4/100

Equipment
Modules: Basic Bridge, Life Support, Small Craft Bridge Add-On.

Statistics
Dim.: 21'×21'×72'   *Payload:* 2.5 tons   *Lwt.:* 75 tons
Volume: 20/50 dtons   *SizeMod:* +6   *Price:* MCr7.7

HP: 4,500

sAccel: 2 Gs empty; see p. 21   *aSpeed:* 1,200

45-TON SLOW CUTTER (RUNABOUT) (TL10)

A smaller version of the modular cutter, the LSP/CU-45 runabout is an unstreamlined version with a 15-ton hull, designed primarily for orbital and intersystem operations.

The slow cutter has a crew of one pilot. It features a sealed body and a single intrinsic coupling for a 30-dton module weighing up to 150 standard tons.

Subassemblies: USL Hull.
Power & Propulsion: 8 Maneuver.
Occupancy: 2 RCS, 2 RS   **Cargo:** 0.5 dtons

Armor	F	RL	B	T	U
All:	4/100	4/100	4/100	4/100	4/100

Equipment
Modules: Accommodations, Cockpit Bridge.

Statistics
Dim.: 21'×21'×69'   *Payload:* 2.5 tons   *Lwt.:* 52 tons
Volume: 15/45 dtons   *SizeMod:* +6   *Price:* MCr5

HP: 3,750

sAccel: 1.5 Gs empty; see p. 21

60-TON FAST CUTTER (SKIFF) (TL10)

A largely unsuccessful design, the LSP/CR-60 skiff was an attempt to improve the performance of the basic cutter. Critics of the design note that the vessel no longer can use the facilities designed for the cutter, as the 30-ton hull is 10 dtons larger. The Navy was uninterested in the design, as the skiff cannot use standard naval launch tubes. The limitations of TL10 drives prevented the performance gains from being very impressive, and only a few companies still manufacture the design.

The fast cutter has a crew of pilot, co-pilot, and engineer. It features a sealed body and a single intrinsic coupling for a 30-dton module weighing up to 240 standard tons.

Subassemblies: SL Hull.
Power & Propulsion: 20 Maneuver.
Occupancy: 5 RCS, 2 RS   **Cargo:** 0.5 dtons

Armor	F	RL	B	T	U
All:	4/100	4/100	4/100	4/100	4/100

Equipment
Modules: Accommodations, Basic Bridge, Small Craft Bridge Add-On.

Statistics
Dim.: 25'×25'×72'   *Payload:* 2.5 tons   *Lwt.:* 109 tons
Volume: 30/60 dtons   *SizeMod:* +7   *Price:* MCr9.5

HP: 6,000

sAccel: 2 Gs empty; see p. 21   *aSpeed:* 1,200

HP: 12,000

sAccel: 1.5 Gs empty; see p. 21   *aSpeed:* 1,000

COLUMBA-CLASS 50-TON ADVANCED CUTTER (TL12)

A newer model of the cutter, the LSP/CM2-50 uses TL12 technology for improved performance. It was constructed at the request of the IISS, but the Imperial Navy has also begun to replace its standard cutters with this design. The advanced cutter offers a heavier load capacity, better performance, and higher comfort. Currently the design is not available to the general public, although that is expected to change soon.

The advanced cutter has a crew of pilot, co-pilot, and engineer. It features a sealed body and heavy compartmentalization, a heavy frame for its hull, and a single intrinsic coupling for a 30-dton module weighing up to 360 standard tons.

Subassemblies: SL Hull.
Power & Propulsion: 11 Maneuver.
Occupancy: 5 RCS, 2 RS   **Cargo:** 0.5 dtons

90-TON MULTI-CUTTER (TL10)

A relatively new design, the LSP/CC-90 multi-cutter is sometimes called a barge, although the term is in disfavor with LSP, which is currently mounting a PR campaign to reinforce the "multi-cutter" name. The craft is a refinement of the ill-fated fast cutter. Engineers noted that the drive configuration of the skiff was capable of moving, slowly, two modules. A redesigned 30-ton body allows two modules to be mounted side-by-side (blocking the inner sides of the modules). The vessel is heavily reinforced, and can operate with two, one, or no modules.

Production of the multi-cutter has begun to pick up, with some commercial outfits using facilities designed for 100-ton shuttles to service the multi-cutters.

The multi-cutter has a crew of pilot, co-pilot, and engineer. It features a sealed body, a heavy frame for its hull, and two intrinsic couplings, each holding a 30-dton module weighing up to 240 standard tons.

Subassemblies: SL Hull.
Power & Propulsion: 20 Maneuver.
Occupancy: 5 RCS, 2 RS   **Cargo:** 0.5 dtons

Armor	F	RL	B	T	U
All:	4/100	4/100	4/100	4/100	4/100

Equipment
Modules: Accommodations, Basic Bridge, Small Craft Bridge Add-On.

Statistics
Dim.: 25′×42′×72′	*Payload:* 2.5 tons	*Lwt.:* 114 tons
Volume: 30/90 dtons	*SizeMod:* +7	*Price:* MCr11.2

Armor	F	RL	B	T	U
All:	4/1,000	4/1,000	4/1,000	4/1,000	4/1,000

Equipment

Modules: Accommodations, hardened Basic Bridge, Small Craft Bridge Add-On, Utility.

Statistics

Dim.: 21′×21′×72' *Payload:* 2.5 tons *Lwt.:* 135 tons
Volume: 20/50 dtons *SizeMod:* +6 *Price:* MCr14.5

HP: 9,000

sAccel: 2 Gs empty; see p. 21 *aSpeed:* 1,200

LOWALAA-CLASS 50-TON ASSAULT CUTTER (TL12)

While several cutter modules are intended for use in ground combat, evaluation of their performance showed that the survival rate of the standard cutter was sub-optimal. When the Imperial Marines began to explore the possibility of using cutters in military operations, LSP promptly developed a modern, heavily armored version of the standard 20-ton hull more suited to the needs of the military. As this design incorporates many military-grade components, a special license is required to purchase the craft. Needless to say, the improved performance of the LSP/CA-50 assault cutter in combat situations has prompted many mercenaries (particularly those equipped with *Broadsword*-class cruisers) to apply for the license.

The assault cutter has a crew of pilot and gunner. It features a sealed body, total compartmentalization, basic stealth, and basic emission cloaking; an extra-heavy frame for its hull; and a single intrinsic coupling with explosive bolts for a 30-dton module weighing up to 720 standard tons.

Subassemblies: SL Hull.
Power & Propulsion: 14 Maneuver.
Occupancy: 2 RS

Armor	F	RL	B	T	U
All:	4/2,000	4/2,000	4/2,000	4/2,000	4/2,000

Weaponry

Laser [Hull:F] +2.

Equipment

Modules: Hardened Cockpit Bridge.

Statistics

Dim.: 21′×21′×72' *Payload:* - *Lwt.:* 203 tons
Volume: 20/50 dtons *SizeMod:* +6 *Price:* MCr24.8

HP: 18,000

sAccel: 2 Gs empty; see p. 21 *aSpeed:* 1,200

SIRIGERKHE-CLASS 50-TON STEALTH CUTTER (TL12)

The newest member of the cutter family, the LSP/CS-50 stealth cutter is largely unknown to the public. The Navy has been its primary user, but the Marines have begun experimenting with using the stealth cutter for covert commando insertions.

The stealth cutter is a marvel of Imperial technology, able to deceive nearly all sensors of a lower TL. Note that if a module with a poorer stealth system is mounted in the stealth cutter's 20-ton hull, the stealth rating of the combined vessel will be that of the module.

The stealth cutter has a crew of pilot and ECM operator. It features a sealed body, heavy compartmentalization, radical stealth, and radical emission cloaking; a heavy frame for its hull; and a single intrinsic coupling for a 30-dton module weighing up to 360 standard tons.

Subassemblies: SL Hull.
Power & Propulsion: 14 Maneuver.
Occupancy: 2 RS

Armor	F	RL	B	T	U
All:	4/500	4/500	4/500	4/500	4/500

Equipment

Modules: Hardened Cockpit Bridge, Jammer.

Statistics

Dim.: 21′×21′×72' *Payload:* - *Lwt.:* 115 tons
Volume: 20/50 dtons *SizeMod:* +6 *Price:* MCr32.8

HP: 18,000

sAccel: 2 Gs empty; see p. 21 *aSpeed:* 1,200

40-ton Hive Federation Modular Pinnace (TL12)

The Hive Federation is also known to employ a variety of modular vessels. A typical example is the modular pinnace, so named because its overall displacement is identical to the Imperial pinnace. Hiver modules displace 25 dtons, rather than the Imperial standard of 30 dtons. Imperial vessels are able to fully use Hiver modules through the use of a "spacer" (see p. 18); Hiver vessels are unable to carry most Imperial modules.

The 15-ton hull of the Hiver pinnace sits on top of its module, rather than the front/back combination of Imperial craft. The modules are also more rectangular than cylindrical – this does not prevent Imperial craft from carrying them (although it looks a bit strange). Unlike Imperial cutters, the Hiver pinnace does not suffer performance loss when operating without a module.

Like most Hiver vessels, the modular pinnace is capable of being operated by a robot brain.

The Hiver pinnace is used in both civilian markets and the Federation Navy. Imports into the Imperium are strictly regulated, due to the military applications and automation levels. Even with the restrictions, the design is in high demand due to its quality construction and performance. Individual pinnaces can be found in the Imperium priced at up to 50% more than the retail value.

The Hive Federation modular pinnace has a crew of pilot, co-pilot, and engineer. It features a sealed body, total compartmentalization, basic stealth, and basic emission cloaking; an extra-heavy robotic frame for its hull; and a single modular coupling for a 25-dton module weighing up to 150 standard tons.

Subassemblies: SL Hull.
Power & Propulsion: 7 Maneuver.
Occupancy: 5 RS

Armor	F	RL	B	T	U
All:	4/500	4/500	4/500	4/500	4/500

Equipment
Modules: Hardened Basic Bridge, Jammer, Small Craft Bridge Add-On, Utility.

Statistics

Dim.: 18′×18′×62′	*Payload:* -	*Lwt.:* 110 tons
Volume: 15/40 dtons	*SizeMod:* +6	*Price:* MCr26.6

HP: 15,000

sAccel: 6.2 Gs empty   *aSpeed:* 3,464

Non-Starships

Modular operations can be extended to cover the in-system transport needs of megacorps and other huge enterprises without losing the "small lot" convenience of the 30-dton module.

Remora-Class 800-ton Modular Lighter (TL10)

A variant of the standard cargo lighter (p. T:FT137), the LSP/LM-800 carries 20 cutter modules along its hull. When using pure cargo modules, the vessel can carry only 480 tons of cargo, compared to the 553 tons of the general cargo lighter. Using the more efficient bulk cargo modules (see p. 46), the modular version can transport 600 tons of freight. In addition, the modular lighter can be loaded and unloaded faster.

The modular lighter has a crew of five: a captain/pilot, navigator/co-pilot, sensors and commo operator/cargomaster, engineer, and mechanic. It features a sealed body; an extra-heavy frame for its hull; and 20 intrinsic couplings for 30-dton modules, each weighing up to 180 standard tons.

Subassemblies: SL Hull.
Power & Propulsion: 102 Maneuver.
Occupancy: 5 RCS, 2RS   **Cargo:** See above

Armor	F	RL	B	T	U
All:	4/100	4/100	4/100	4/100	4/100

Equipment
Modules: Accommodations, Basic Bridge, Engineering, 53 Vehicle Bay (50-ton modular cutter).

Statistics

Dim.: 32′×62′×200′	*Payload:* 75 tons	*Lwt.:* 792 tons
Volume: 200/800 dtons	*SizeMod:* +8	*Price:* MCr34.5

HP: 90,000

sAccel: 0.5 Gs *aSpeed:* 500

Starships

Many commercial enterprises attempt to profitably extend modular operations across the stars, especially on trade mains where a given consignment of cargo might have 200 distinct destinations. In such circumstances, efficiencies lost in transit often can be made up in cargo handling.

Naakil-Class 100-ton Jump Cutter (TL10)

This small vessel is equipped to carry a pair of 30-ton modules through jump space. It has been a moderately successful design, although it is not a cost-effective way of transporting modules, bulk transports being more efficient.

The jump cutter has a crew of two, the pilot/navigator and engineer. It features a sealed body; a heavy frame for its hull; and two intrinsic couplings for 30-dton modules, each weighing up to 300 tons.

Subassemblies: SL Hull.
Power & Propulsion: 11 Maneuver, 2 Jump.
Fuel: 10 Fuel.
Occupancy: 1-4   **Cargo:** 0.5 dtons

Armor	F	RL	B	T	U
All:	4/100	4/100	4/100	4/100	4/100

Equipment
Modules: Basic Bridge, Engineering, Stateroom, Utility.

Statistics
Dim.: 21′×21′×115′   *Payload:* 2.5 tons   *Lwt.:* 127 tons
Volume: 40/100 dtons *SizeMod:* +7   *Price:* MCr16

HP: 15,000

sAccel: 3.5 Gs *Jump:* 1   *aSpeed:* 2,450

MODULAR SHIP SERIES

Building on the success of the original cutter, LSP extended the modular concept to larger vessels, with limited success among merchant users. For a given tonnage, a modular vessel will have more wasted space than a standard hull, and the flexibility offered by modules doesn't always translate into profit. However, the line found its niche in the private and scientific sectors, which have never been primarily concerned with economic performance. Many universities use modular vessels as laboratory ships, since their mission can be readily changed. Ling originally offered six different models: three hull sizes with two jump performances each. The Modular Ship Medium (10-module) Jump-1 version was the only truly successful one, and is still being manufactured, but any of the others might be found second (or third, or fourth) hand. Ling built them to last.

It should be noted that none of these vessels carries enough fuel for a jump – it is assumed that one or more fuel modules will be carried.

Ling MSL-J1 (TL10)

This ship is perfectly serviceable, but not efficient enough for mercantile use. As such, it is more popular with universities and research organizations than commercial shipping companies.

The MSL-J1 has a crew of five: captain/pilot, navigator, sensors/commo operator, and two engineers. It features a sealed body; a heavy frame for its hull; and three intrinsic couplings for 30-dton modules, each weighing up to 240 tons. The 2.5 "waste" spaces in the drive room and 3 unused spaces in the turret could be used as non-modular cargo holds. The given statistics assume one fuel module and two cargo modules are carried, with no cargo in the ship proper. The ship's empty G rating exceeds its safe limit of 2.5 Gs carrying no modules or 3 Gs carrying one or two modules.

Subassemblies: USL Hull, Turret +5.
Power & Propulsion: 15 Maneuver, 4 Jump.
Fuel: See above.
Occupancy: 5-10   **Cargo:** 5.5 dtons

Armor	F	RL	B	T	U
All:	4/100	4/100	4/100	4/100	4/100

Equipment
Modules: Basic Bridge, Engineering, 5 Stateroom, Utility, 53 Vehicle Bay (50-ton modular cutter).

Statistics
Dim.: 42′×42′×54′   *Payload:* 409 tons   *Lwt.:* 589 tons
Volume: 100/190 dtons *SizeMod:* +8   *Price:* MCr21.5

HP: 30,000 [Hull] 1,200 [Tur]

sAccel: 1 G/3.3 Gs empty   *Jump:* 1

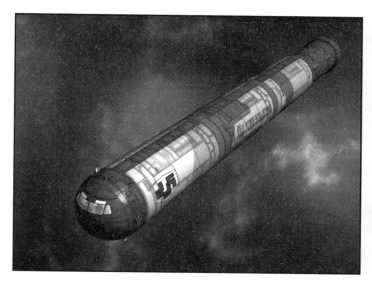

Ling MSL-J2 (TL10)

This version is less popular than the Jump-1 version, since two fuel modules are required to fully utilize its jump capacity, leaving but one for any cargo required by its mission.

The MSL-J2 has a crew of five: captain/pilot, navigator, sensors/commo operator, and two engineers. It features a sealed body; a heavy frame for its hull; and three intrinsic couplings for 30-dton modules, each weighing up to 240 tons. The 0.5 "waste" spaces in the drive room and 3 unused spaces in the turret could be used as non-modular cargo holds. The given statistics assume two fuel modules and one cargo module are carried, with no cargo in the ship proper. The ship's empty G rating exceeds its safe limit of 2.5 Gs carrying no modules or 3 Gs carrying one or two modules.

Subassemblies: USL Hull, Turret +5.
Power & Propulsion: 15 Maneuver, 6 Jump.
Fuel: See above.
Occupancy: 5-10   **Cargo:** 3.5 dtons

Armor	F	RL	B	T	U
All:	4/100	4/100	4/100	4/100	4/100

Equipment
Modules: Basic Bridge, Engineering, 5 Stateroom, Utility, 53 Vehicle Bay (50-ton modular cutter).

Statistics
Dim.: 42′×42′×54′   *Payload:* 309 tons   *Lwt.:* 497 tons
Volume: 100/190 dtons *SizeMod:* +8   *Price:* MCr27.7

HP: 30,000 [Hull] 1,200 [Tur]

sAccel: 1.2 Gs/3.1 Gs empty   *Jump:* 2

Ling MSM-J1 (TL10)

The Ling MSM-J1 is still in production, and often found in the hands of free traders. It has a crew of six: captain/pilot, navigator, sensors operator, commo operator, and two engineers. It features a sealed body; an extra-heavy frame for its hull; and 10 intrinsic couplings for 30-dton modules, each weighing up to 240 tons. The hull includes 6.5 hold spaces; in addition, the 5 "waste" spaces in the drive room and 6 unused spaces in the turrets could be used as non-modular cargo holds. The given statistics assume two fuel modules and eight cargo modules are carried, with no cargo in the ship proper. The MSM-J1's empty G rating exceeds its safe limit of 2 Gs carrying 0-1 modules, 2.5 Gs carrying 2-4 modules, or 3 Gs carrying 5-9 modules.

Subassemblies: SL Hull, 2 Turrets +5.
Power & Propulsion: 49 Maneuver, 10 Jump.
Fuel: 6 Fuel and see above.
Occupancy: 6-12   **Cargo:** 17.5 dtons

Armor	F	RL	B	T	U
All:	4/100	4/100	4/100	4/100	4/100

Equipment
Modules: Basic Bridge, Engineering, 6 Stateroom, Utility, 53 Vehicle Bay (50-ton modular cutter).

Statistics
Dim.: 42'×63'×190'   *Payload:* 1,369 tons   *Lwt.:* 1,762 tons
Volume: 200/500 dtons *SizeMod:* +8   *Price:* MCr55.8

HP: 90,000 [Hull] 1,200 [each Tur]

sAccel: 1.1 Gs/4.9 Gs empty   *Jump:* 1   *aSpeed:* 2,248

Ling MSM-J2 (TL10)

The added expense and decreased useful payload of the MSM-J2 medium ship (compared to the MSM-J1) have made it fairly unpopular, and the vessel is no longer in production. However, used ones are fairly easy to find and parts are not a problem, being interchangeable with other MS series ships.

The MSM-J2 requires a crew of seven: captain/pilot, navigator, sensors operator, commo operator, and three engineers. It features a sealed body; an extra-heavy frame for its hull; and 10 intrinsic couplings for 30-dton modules, each weighing up to 240 tons. The hull includes 0.5 hold spaces; in addition, the 6 unused spaces in the turrets could be used as non-modular cargo holds. The given statistics assume four fuel modules and six cargo modules are carried, with no cargo in the ship proper. The ship's empty G rating exceeds its safe limit of 2 Gs carrying 0-1 modules, 2.5 Gs carrying 2-4 modules, or 3 Gs carrying 5-9 modules.

Subassemblies: SL Hull, 2 Turrets +5.
Power & Propulsion: 49 Maneuver, 15 Jump.
Fuel: 12 Fuel and see above.
Occupancy: 6-12   **Cargo:** 6.5 dtons

Armor	F	RL	B	T	U
All:	4/100	4/100	4/100	4/100	4/100

Equipment
Modules: Basic Bridge, Engineering, 6 Stateroom, Utility, 53 Vehicle Bay (50-ton modular cutter).

Statistics
Dim.: 42'×63'×190'   *Payload:* 1,161 tons   *Lwt.:* 1,582 tons
Volume: 200/500 dtons *SizeMod:* +8   *Price:* MCr72.3

HP: 90,000 [Hull] 1,200 [each Tur]

sAccel: 1.2 Gs/4.6 Gs empty   *Jump:* 2   *aSpeed:* 2,248

"Frankly, I think the main reason the Modular Cutter is so popular is that people like to collect the action figures. The Ling CM-50 basic playset has been a top seller for years."

– Leonard Pokryfki,
Marketing Director,
Warehouse 2300 Inc.

Ling MSH-J1 (TL10)

The "Modular Ship, Heavy" has had some success as a configurable mercenary cruiser, although the jump performance of both models is inferior to most other designs. Surface-area limitations make it more efficient for the MSH to carry its modules internally. It can carry 24 modules in all by leaving two aboard the pair of modular cutters that the ship also carries.

The MSH-J1 has a crew of eight: captain, pilot, navigator, sensors operator, commo operator, and three engineers. It features a sealed body. Apart from modules, the ship can carry 0.5 tons of cargo in its holds, 10 more in its spare drive-room space, and 30 in its empty turrets. The given statistics assume five fuel modules and 19 cargo modules, with no cargo in the ship proper.

Subassemblies: USL Hull, 10 Turrets +5.
Power & Propulsion: 80 Maneuver, 20 Jump.
Fuel: 0; see above.
Occupancy: 8-32   **Cargo:** 40.5 dtons

Armor	F	RL	B	T	U
All:	4/100	4/100	4/100	4/100	4/100

Equipment
Modules: Basic Bridge, Engineering, 16 Stateroom, 2 Utility, 22×32 Vehicle Bay (22 30-ton modules), 2×53 Vehicle Bay (2 50-ton modular cutters).

Statistics
Dim.: 35'×70'×205'   *Payload:* 3,169 tons   *Lwt.:* 3,871 tons
Volume: 1,000 dtons   *SizeMod:* +10   *Price:* MCr85

HP: 60,000 [Hull] 1,200 [each Tur]

sAccel: 0.8 Gs/4.5 Gs empty   *Jump:* 1

Ling MSH-J2 (TL10)

This ship is considered slightly more practical than the J1 version, due to its increased range. It is also rarer, because so many went in harm's way. The MSH-J2 has a crew of nine: captain, pilot, navigator, sensors operator, commo operator, and four engineers. Apart from modules, the ship has a 0.5-ton hold and can carry 30 tons of cargo in its empty turrets. The given statistics assume 10 fuel modules and 14 cargo modules, with no cargo in the ship proper. It features a sealed body.

Subassemblies: USL Hull, 10 Turrets +5.

Power & Propulsion: 80 Maneuver, 30 Jump.

Fuel: 0; see above.

Occupancy: 9-32   **Cargo:** 30 dtons

Armor	F	RL	B	T	U
All:	4/100	4/100	4/100	4/100	4/100

Equipment

Modules: Basic Bridge, Engineering, 16 Stateroom, 2 Utility, 22×32 Vehicle Bay (22 30-ton modules), 2×53 Vehicle Bay (2 50-ton modular cutters).

Statistics

Dim.: 35'×70'×205'   *Payload:* 2,729 tons   *Lwt.:* 3,471 tons
Volume: 1,000 dtons   *SizeMod:* +10   *Price:* MCr116

HP: 60,000 [Hull] 1,200 [each Tur]

sAccel: 0.9 Gs/4.3 Gs empty   *Jump:* 2

K Series Modular Frame (TL12)

The "'K-frame" was GSbAG's attempt to get in on the modular act with a *fully* modular spacecraft. The basic hull is a shell containing nothing but grapples, airlocks, and connecting passages. It doesn't become a ship until modules are attached.

Each frame, from K-3 to K-30, is rated by the maximum number of modules that it can hold. Each frame also has a maximum drive module capacity. Thus, the K-5 can mount four non-drive modules plus a drive module, or three non-drive modules and two drives, but not two non-drive modules and three drives. Of course, a hull can mount fewer modules than the maximum. To round off the displacement, several frames have waste space that can be used as storage or cargo space.

A K-frame will mount any standard module of 250 stons or less. However, to avoid compatibility problems, the K series requires that every module mounted be self-powered and provide the necessary life support. The dedicated K-series drive and bridge modules are described on p. 64. Only data and control information is shared between modules, using standard Imperial protocols.

Since each module that requires power must supply its own, a K-frame ship is more complex and expensive than a regular hull. They proved to be poor economic performers along the mains, but are still in production for frontier locations where their versatility offsets their flaws.

Each frame contains the listed number of grapples (rated at 250 standard tons each), airlocks, cargo space, and a DR 100 hull. The frames are all unstreamlined.

Max No. Modules	Full Dis-placemt	Max No. Drives	Air Locks	Cargo Space	Frame Weight	Frame Cost	HP
3	100	1	1	3	85.6	6.81	2,631
4	130	2	1	1	111.3	8.31	2,631
5	165	2	1	4	138.3	9.91	3,449
6	195	3	1	2	164.0	11.21	3,449
7	225	3	1	0	189.6	12.61	3,449
8	260	4	1	3	216.3	14.01	4,178
9	290	4	2	0	244.9	15.22	4,178
10	325	5	2	3	271.4	16.62	4,848
11	355	5	2	1	297.0	17.82	4,848
12	390	6	2	4	323.4	19.12	5,474
13	420	6	2	2	348.9	20.32	5,474
14	450	6	2	0	374.4	21.42	5,474
15	485	6	2	3	400.8	22.72	6,066
16	515	7	2	1	426.2	23.82	6,066
17	550	7	3	3	455.5	25.03	6,632
18	580	7	3	1	480.9	26.13	6,632
19	615	7	3	4	507.3	27.33	7,173
20	645	8	3	2	532.7	28.33	7,173
21	675	8	3	0	558.1	29.53	7,173
22	710	8	3	3	584.3	30.53	7,695
23	740	8	3	1	609.8	61.63	7,695
24	775	9	3	4	635.8	32.73	8,199
25	805	9	4	1	664.3	33.74	8,199
26	840	9	4	4	690.4	34.94	8,690
27	870	9	4	2	715.8	35.94	8,690
28	900	10	4	0	741.2	36.94	8,690
29	935	10	4	3	767.3	38.04	9,165
30	965	10	4	1	792.7	38.94	9,165

Shidar-Class 2,000-ton Modular Frigate (TL12)

An experimental design in the Imperial Navy, the *Shidar* class is just beginning its combat trials. It is expected to perform below the standards of existing vessels, but have superior versatility due to its modular construction. No weapons are initially installed on the vessel, but an appropriate selection can be mounted in rapid time at a naval base.

The *Shidar* has a crew of 36: the captain, executive officer, pilot, navigator, active sensor operator, passive sensor operator, commo operator, computer officer, three medics, two stewards, six cutter crew personnel, five engineers, and 12 gunners. The stewards, four engineers, and 10 gunners are double-bunked. It features total compartmentalization, sealed body, radical stealth, and radical emission cloaking. The "base" ship mounts no weapons – these are installed (or the turrets and bay used as hold space) depending on mission needs, just as with its modules. The given statistics assume that it carries two Advanced Fuel and 14 Advanced Cargo modules.

Subassemblies: USL Hull, 10 Turrets +5, 1 Bay +7.

Power & Propulsion: 391 Maneuver, 100 Jump.

Fuel: 800 Fuel.

Occupancy: See above   **Cargo:** See above

Armor	F	RL	B	T	U
All:	4/2,000	4/2,000	4/2,000	4/2,000	4/2,000

Equipment

Modules: Hardened Command Bridge, 2 Engineering, Information Center, 30 Stateroom, 4 Utility, 14×32 Vehicle Bay (14 30-ton modules), 2×53 Vehicle Bay (2 50-ton modular cutters).

Statistics

Dim.: 100′×100′×100′ *Payload:* 3,388 tons *Lwt.:* 9,622 tons
Volume: 2,000 dtons *SizeMod:* +10 *Price:* MCr836

HP: 90,000 [Hull]   1,200 [each Tur]   9,750 [Bay]

sAccel: 4 Gs/6.2 Gs empty   *Jump:* 4

KODRIIK-CLASS 5,000-TON JUMP SHIP (TL12)

The poor reception for its modular series of ships prompted LSP to re-evaluate the effectiveness of modular starships. Noting the successful design points of LASH tenders, LSP's follow-on effort attempts to combine the versatility of a modular vessel with improved economic performance.

The *Kodriik* is a jump-6 starship with a large external grapple. It carries cargo in special 1,000-dton modules, forming a train of one to five of them. Each carried module reduces the jump performance of the *Kodriik* by 1 parsec.

A *Kodriik* carrying five modules is only capable of jump-1, but is highly configurable and can operate much in the same manner as a LASH tender and its subordinate vessels. Each jump module is a distinct non-starship, able to operate on its own. It also provides grapples for the next pod in the line. See pp. 64-65 for a list of available jump modules.

The *Kodriik* has a crew of 32: the captain, executive officer, two pilots, two navigators, two commo operators, two sensors operators, two computer operators, two medics, four stewards, six engineers, two cargomasters, and six mechanics. It features a sealed body.

Subassemblies: SL Hull.

Power & Propulsion: 100 Maneuver, 350 Jump.

Fuel: 3,000 Fuel.

Occupancy: See above   **Cargo:** 300 dtons

Armor	F	RL	B	T	U
All:	4/100	4/100	4/100	4/100	4/100

Equipment

Modules: Command Bridge, 3 Engineering, 52 External Grapple, 16 Fuel Processor, 41 Stateroom, 10 Utility.

Statistics

Dim.: 50′×80′×625′ *Payload:* 1,500 tons *Lwt.:* 8,370 tons
Volume: 5,000 dtons *SizeMod:* +11 *Price:* MCr1,667.2

HP: 165,000

sAccel: 1.4 Gs/1.1 Gs empty   *Jump:* 6   *aSpeed:* 2,605

50-TON MODULAR CUTTER (TL10)

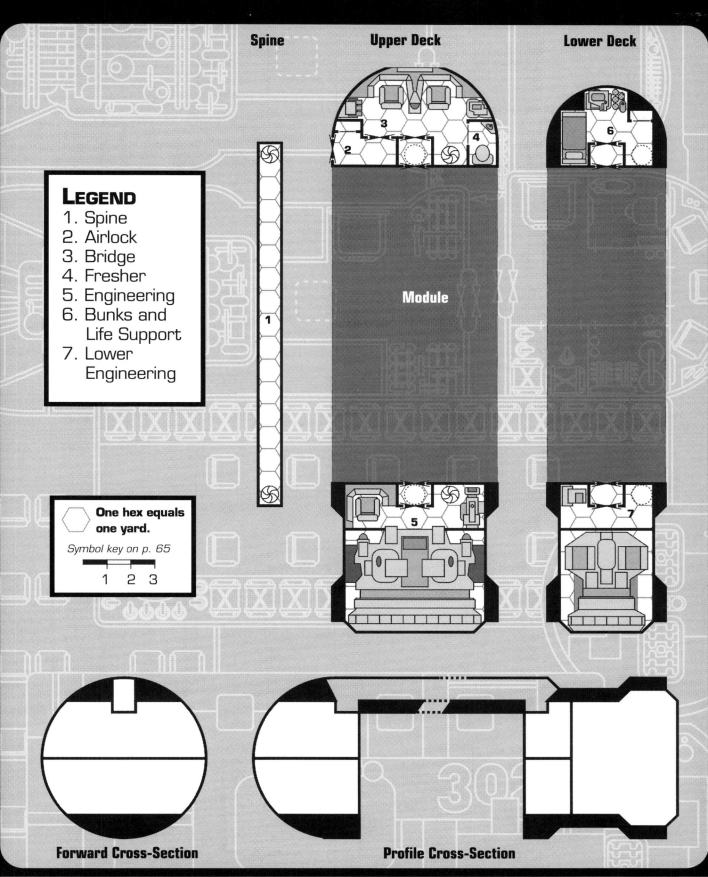

Spine

Upper Deck

Lower Deck

LEGEND
1. Spine
2. Airlock
3. Bridge
4. Fresher
5. Engineering
6. Bunks and
   Life Support
7. Lower
   Engineering

Module

One hex equals
one yard.

Symbol key on p. 65

1   2   3

Forward Cross-Section

Profile Cross-Section

45-ton Slow Cutter (Runabout) (TL10) and 90-ton Multi-Cutter (Barge) (TL10)

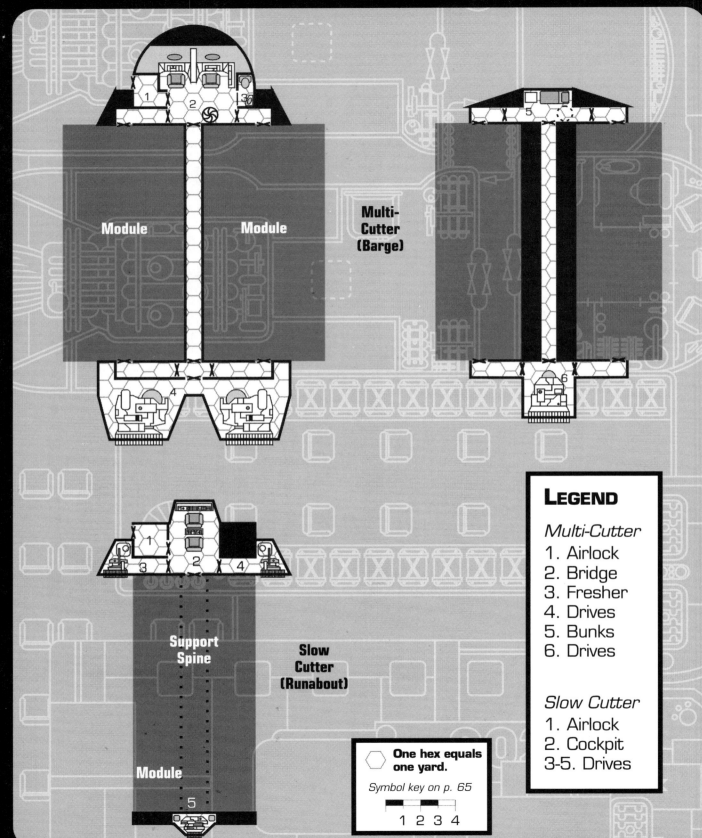

Module   Module

Multi-Cutter (Barge)

Support Spine

Slow Cutter (Runabout)

Module

LEGEND

Multi-Cutter
1. Airlock
2. Bridge
3. Fresher
4. Drives
5. Bunks
6. Drives

Slow Cutter
1. Airlock
2. Cockpit
3-5. Drives

One hex equals one yard.

Symbol key on p. 65

1 2 3 4

60-TON FAST CUTTER (SKIFF) (TL10)

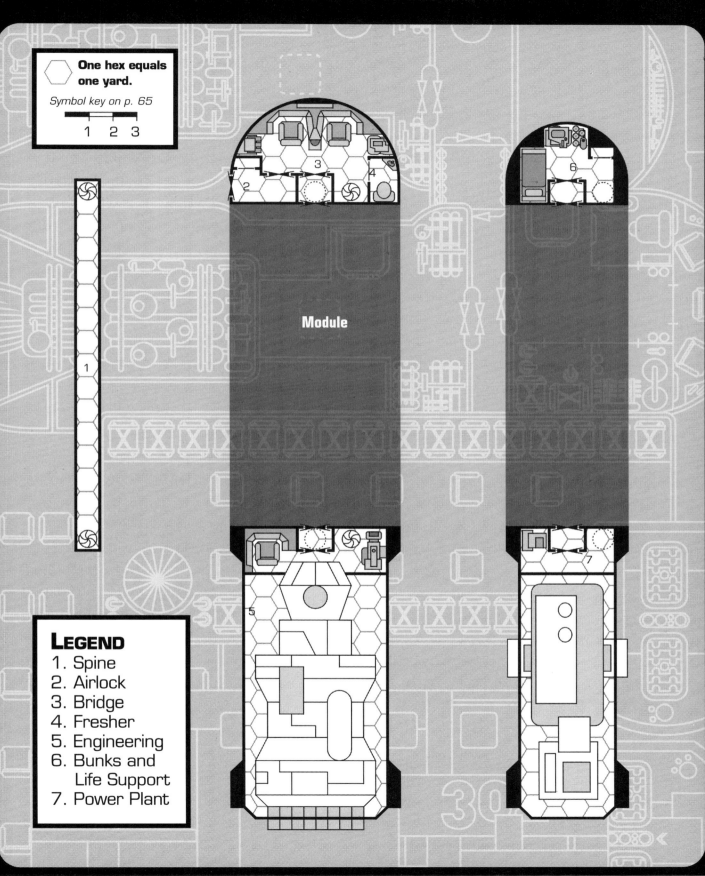

One hex equals one yard.

Symbol key on p. 65

1 2 3

Module

LEGEND

1. Spine
2. Airlock
3. Bridge
4. Fresher
5. Engineering
6. Bunks and Life Support
7. Power Plant

COLUMBA-CLASS 50-TON ADVANCED CUTTER (TL12)

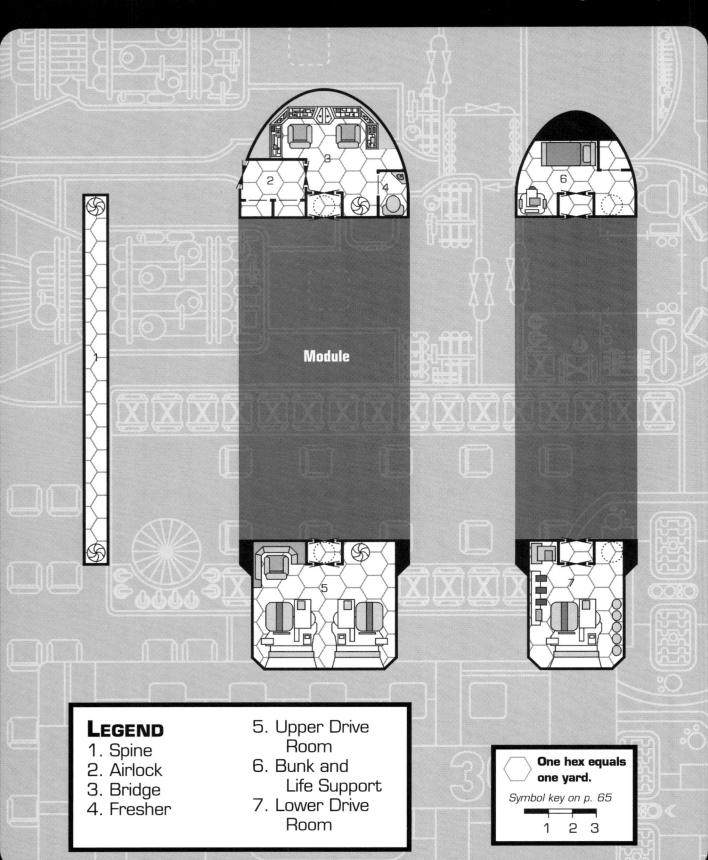

LEGEND
1. Spine
2. Airlock
3. Bridge
4. Fresher
5. Upper Drive Room
6. Bunk and Life Support
7. Lower Drive Room

One hex equals one yard.

Symbol key on p. 65

1 2 3

Module

1 2 3 4 5 6 7

Module

1 2 3

Module

Module

EQUIPMENT, VEHICLES, AND VESSELS

LOWALAA-CLASS 50-TON ASSAULT CUTTER (TL12)

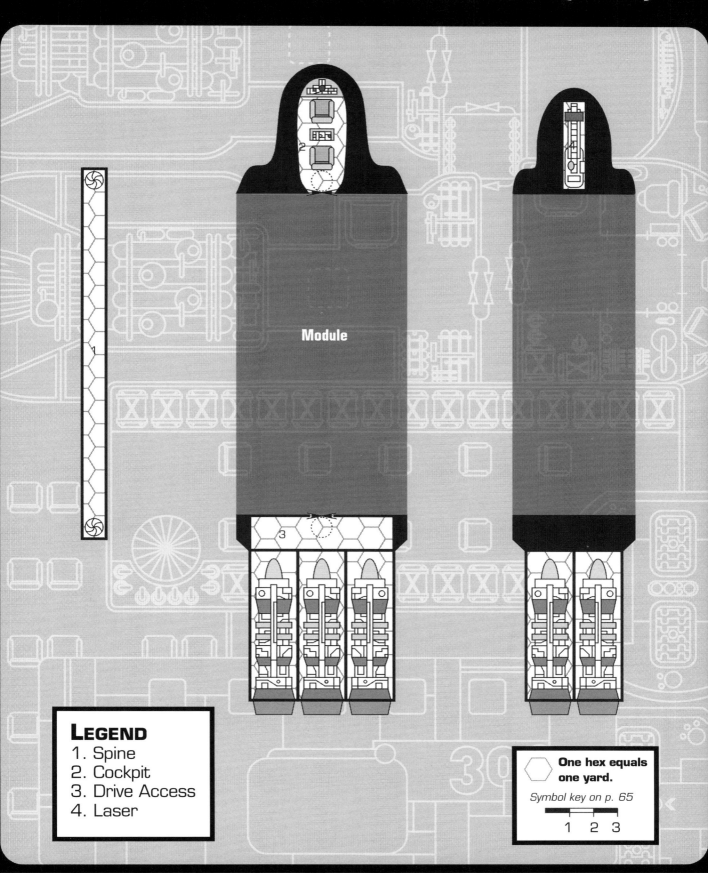

Module

LEGEND
1. Spine
2. Cockpit
3. Drive Access
4. Laser

One hex equals one yard.

Symbol key on p. 65

1   2   3

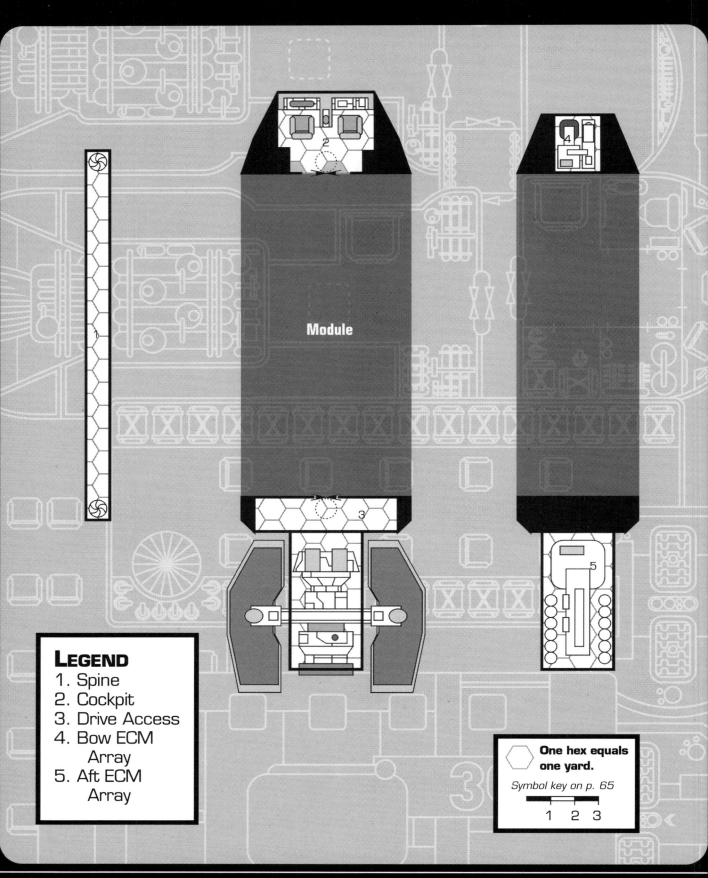

Module

LEGEND
1. Spine
2. Cockpit
3. Drive Access
4. Bow ECM
    Array
5. Aft ECM
    Array

One hex equals one yard.

Symbol key on p. 65

1 2 3

NAAKIL-CLASS 100-TON JUMP CUTTER

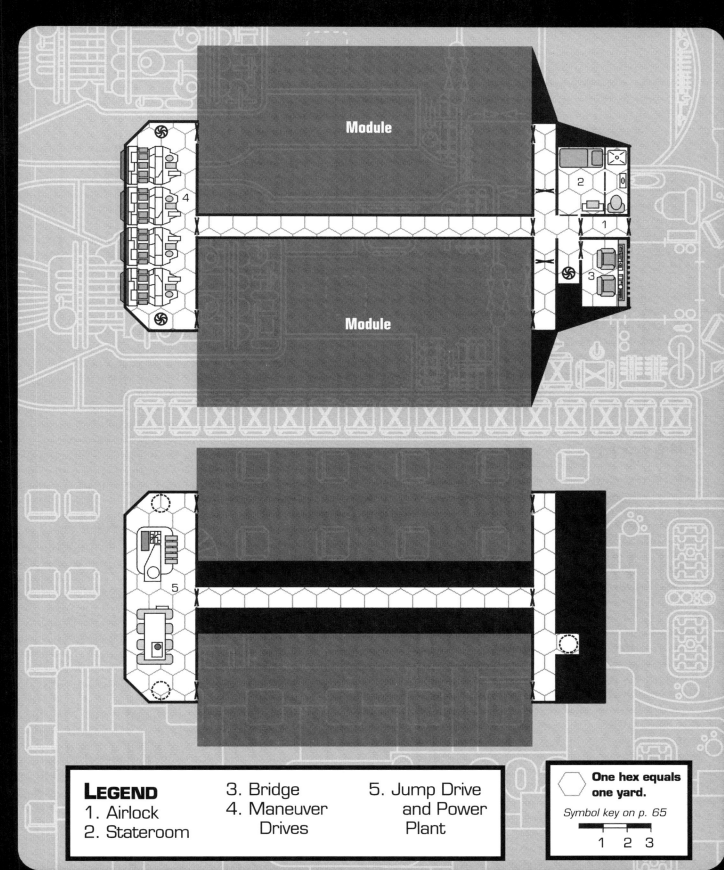

Module

Module

LEGEND
1. Airlock
2. Stateroom
3. Bridge
4. Maneuver Drives
5. Jump Drive and Power Plant

One hex equals one yard.

Symbol key on p. 65

1 2 3

Pinnace

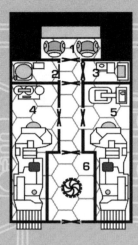

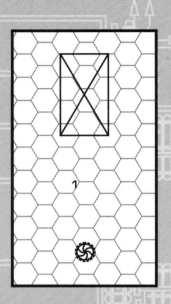

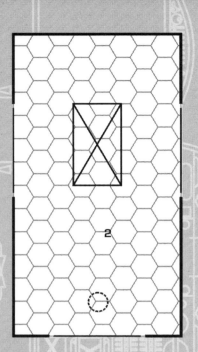

Hiver Cargo

PINNACE LEGEND

1. Bridge
2. Fresher
3. Life Support
4-5. Drives
6. Airlock

Hiver Passenger

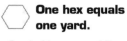

One hex equals one yard.

Symbol key on p. 65

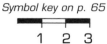

1 2 3

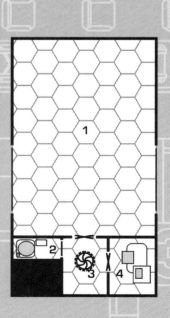

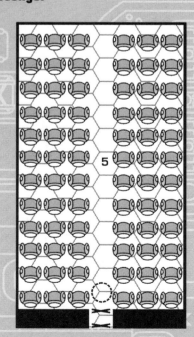

MODULE LEGEND

Hiver Cargo
1. Upper Cargo Bay
2. Lower Cargo Bay

Hiver Passenger
1. Cargo Bay
2. Fresher
3. Airlock
4. Life Support

Hiver Embassy
1. Stateroom
2. Engineering and Life Support
3. Galley
4. Stateroom
5. Common Area
6. Air/Raft Bay
7-8. Offices
9. Communications Bay
10. Airlock

Hiver War
1. Troop Seating
2. Fresher
3. Airlock
4. Battledress Morgue
5. Engineering and Life Support
6. Sickbay
7. Command Center
8. Assault Entry Lock
9. Drop-Capsule Storage and Launchers
10. Vehicle Bay

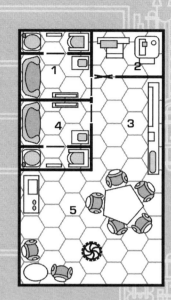

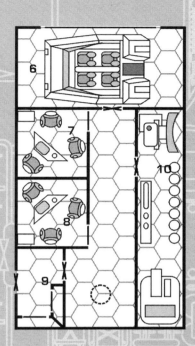

Hiver Embassy

Hiver War

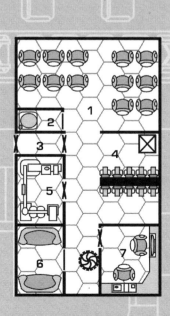

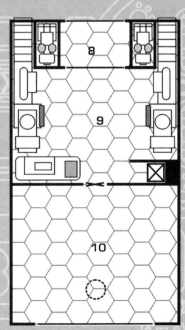

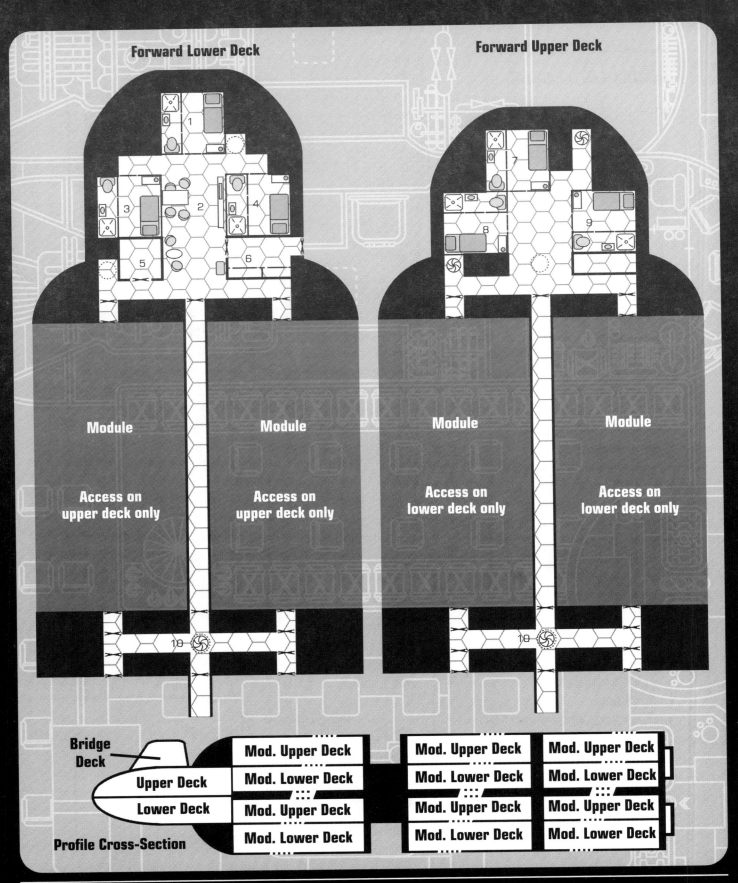

Forward Lower Deck

Forward Upper Deck

Module

Access on upper deck only

Module

Access on upper deck only

Module

Access on lower deck only

Module

Access on lower deck only

Bridge Deck

Upper Deck

Lower Deck

Profile Cross-Section

Mod. Upper Deck	Mod. Upper Deck	Mod. Upper Deck
Mod. Lower Deck	Mod. Lower Deck	Mod. Lower Deck
Mod. Upper Deck	Mod. Upper Deck	Mod. Upper Deck
Mod. Lower Deck	Mod. Lower Deck	Mod. Lower Deck

Bridge Deck

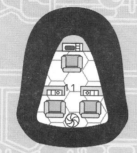

Rear Deck
(two levels, identical except
for module access)

Module

Module

10

Lower module has
upper deck access;
upper module has
lower deck access

Lower module has
upper deck access;
upper module has
lower deck access

One hex equals
one yard.

Scale in yards

1   2   3

Symbol key on p. 65

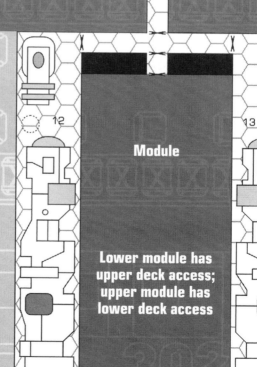

Module

12

13

Lower module has
upper deck access;
upper module has
lower deck access

LEGEND
1. Stateroom
2. Common Area
3-4. Staterooms
5. Cargo Bay
6. Airlock
7-9. Stateroom
10. Turret Access
11. Bridge
12-13. Engineering

Modules

This chapter contains a selection of modules and pallets for use with the various models of modular craft. It should be noted that these are only a few of the more common modules; thousands of different types of specialized modules exist.

STANDARD MODULE VARIANTS

Several of the listed modules have variants that are designed to better interact with cutters other than the standard 50-dton modular cutter. These variants are:

Advanced: An advanced module has its TL upgraded to 12, its compartmentalization upgraded to heavy, and its armor upgraded to DR 1,000.

Armored: An armored module has its TL upgraded to 12, its stealth upgraded to basic, its emission cloaking upgraded to basic, its compartmentalization upgraded to total, its frame upgraded to extra-heavy, giving it 24,000 hit points, and its armor upgraded to DR 2,000.

Stealth: A stealth variant has its TL upgraded to 12, its stealth upgraded to radical, its emission cloaking upgraded to radical, its compartmentalization upgraded to heavy, and its armor upgraded to DR 500.

STANDARD MODULES AND PALLETS

See p. 7 for the distinction between modules and pallets.

BOARDING (TL12)

This module is designed to deliver up to 48 marines to an enemy spacecraft or space station and act as a staging area for boarding actions. The module possesses strong grappling arms that can reach out and forcefully clamp to the target hull, while a bank of fusion torches make quick work of the thickest armor. A battledress morgue is provided for maintenance, and the sickbays allow for wounded to be treated at the LZ (the term is still used for the primary assault point, even if it is no longer strictly accurate).

This module has no crew. It features total compartmentalization, sealed body, basic stealth, and basic emission cloaking.

Subassemblies: SL Hull.
Occupancy: 24 RS   **Cargo:** 5 dtons

Armor	F	RL	B	T	U
All:	4/2,000	4/2,000	4/2,000	4/2,000	4/2,000

Equipment
Modules: 3 Boarding Clamp, Engineering, 2 Hull Cutter, 2 Large Entry, 6 Maneuver, 2 Morgue, 2 Passenger, 4 Sickbay, Utility.

Statistics
Dim.: 21'×21'×42'   *Payload:* 50 tons   *Lwt.:* 294 tons
Volume: 30 dtons   *SizeMod:* +7   *Price:* MCr23.1

HP: 24,000

BULK CARGO (TL10)

A large pallet capable of carrying up to seven 4C cargo containers, the bulk cargo pallet can be used by in-system cargo cutters for intersystem transport, but is more often employed by large modular freighters.

The bulk-cargo-rack pallet has no crew.

Subassemblies: USL Hull.
Cargo: 0 (28) dtons

Armor	F	RL	B	T	U
All:	4/100	4/100	4/100	4/100	4/100

Equipment
Modules: Vehicle Bay holding 7 4-ton standard cargo containers.

Statistics
Dim.: 21'×21'×42'   *Payload:* 140 tons   *Lwt.:* 165 tons
Volume: 30 dtons   *SizeMod:* +7   *Price:* MCr0.4

HP: 6,000

CARGO (TL10)

The basic cutter module, the cargo unit is the basis for hundreds of variants. The simple cutter module is a two-deck cylinder with four cargo hatches, two on each deck. Variants included wide-open single-deck units, or units optimized for specific types of cargo (grain, livestock, liquids, etc.). The cargo module is highly customizable, with slots in the floor and walls accepting partitions and non-load-bearing walls.

The cargo module has no crew. It possesses a sealed body.

Subassemblies: SL Hull.
Cargo: 24 dtons

Armor	F	RL	B	T	U
All:	4/100	4/100	4/100	4/100	4/100

Statistics
Dim.: 21′×21′×42′   *Payload:* 120 tons   *Lwt.:* 144 tons
Volume: 30 dtons   *SizeMod:* +7   *Price:* MCr0.7

HP: 6,000

Advanced

See p. 46. LWt. becomes 202, Price MCr1.4.

Armored

See p. 46. Lwt. becomes 287, Price MCr4.9.

Stealth

See p. 46. Lwt. becomes 166, Price MCr7.

CLASS I STARPORT (TL10)

An example of a starport module, the Jiratech S-6500 can perform all of the basic functions of a Class I starport. The basic bridge represents the control center, with radios and sensors to guide in approaching craft. The single office serves as a customs station as well as administration services. This module is unique due to the presence of a sickbay, a useful perk on worlds with less than hospitable conditions. The starport is capable of being operated by a single individual – in these cases, some starport "managers" make some extra money by renting out the extra two staterooms as hotel rooms. Note that the S-6500 has no utility module. While it can be operated as an orbital station, the personnel will be in weightless conditions. Other models are available that provide gravity.

The Class I starport module has no crew. It features a sealed body.

Subassemblies: SL Hull.
Occupancy: See above   **Cargo:** 3.5 dtons

Armor	F	RL	B	T	U
All:	4/100	4/100	4/100	4/100	4/100

Equipment
Modules: Basic Bridge, Engineering, Office, Sickbay, 3 Staterooms.

Statistics
Dim.: 21′×21′×42′   *Payload:* 18 tons   *Lwt.:* 66 tons
Volume: 30 dtons   *SizeMod:* +7   *Price:* MCr5.3

HP: 6,000

COMMUTER (TL10)

The commuter module is intended for passenger transport on a mass-transit scale – 260 individuals can be carried in cramped but comfortable accommodations. In order to make the journey as pleasant as possible, gravity is provided. No cargo space is available other than overhead compartments capable of holding a small briefcase. Commuter pods are often used to shuttle people between the high and low ports of a starport.

The commuter module has a crew of four stewards. It features a sealed body.

Subassemblies: SL Hull.
Occupancy: 264 RS

Armor	F	RL	B	T	U
All:	4/100	4/100	4/100	4/100	4/100

Equipment
Modules: Engineering, 22 Passenger, Utility.

Statistics
Dim.: 21′×21′×42′   *Payload:* -   *Lwt.:* 51 tons
Volume: 30 dtons   *SizeMod:* +7   *Price:* MCr3

HP: 6,000

CONTAINERIZED CARGO (TL10)

This module is slotted to allow two standard cargo racks to be loaded (each holding two 4C containers). There is significant waste space in this model, causing some to discount its usefulness. However, this design is extremely efficient in loading and unloading operations – a great deal of time can be saved. And some merchants believe in the credo "time is money." Winches are provided to assist in loading.

The containerized-cargo module has no crew. It features a sealed body.

Subassemblies: SL Hull.
Cargo: 2 (+18) dtons

Armor	F	RL	B	T	U
All:	4/100	4/100	4/100	4/100	4/100

Equipment
Modules: 2 Vehicle Bays (each holding up to 9-dton cargo rack), 2 Winch.

Statistics
Dim.: 21'×21'×42'	*Payload:* 110 tons	*Lwt.:* 147 tons
Volume: 30 dtons	*SizeMod:* +7	*Price:* MCr0.9

HP: 6,000

CUSTOMS (TL10)

A basic design intended to serve as a customs and inspection module. Since the cutter is not a high-performance craft, this version is not intended to pursue suspected violators, thus it is not armed, nor does it possess large prisoner facilities. However, it is an excellent design for simple merchant inspections and police duties.

The customs module has a crew of one or more, depending on mission needs. It features a sealed body.

Subassemblies: SL Hull.
Occupancy: See Modules   **Cargo:** 6 dtons

Armor	F	RL	B	T	U
All:	4/100	4/100	4/100	4/100	4/100

Equipment
Modules: Brig, Bunkroom, Sickbay, 2 Staterooms, Utility.

Statistics
Dim.: 21'×21'×42'	*Payload:* 30 tons	*Lwt.:* 87 tons
Volume: 30 dtons	*SizeMod:* +7	*Price:* MCr1.3

HP: 6,000

ECM (TL12)

An incredible array of electronics packs the hull of this module. When used with the stealth cutter, this gives the Imperial Navy a potent electronic-warfare platform. The probe bay is usually fitted with sensor drones and wild-weasel decoys. The single missile turret carries a collection of ECM and HARM missiles to jam and destroy enemy sensors. The information

"I spent two years living in a 'collapse-a-base' during my time as a graduate student, and the only major problem I encountered was that you have to be very careful to police the lavatory before folding the place for transit – they don't always run the artificial gravity in those things when they move them, and messy accidents can occur if they are not properly secured."

– Anton Wilson Peale

center and additional computer banks are able to process an immense amount of digital information, allowing the craft to pierce nearly any stealth technology. The vessel is so crowded that only a single stateroom is provided for breaks.

The ECM module has a crew of four EW specialists. It features total compartmentalization, a sealed body, radical stealth, and radical emission cloaking.

Subassemblies: SL Hull.
Occupancy: 4   **Cargo:** 2 dtons

Armor	F	RL	B	T	U
All:	4/500	4/500	4/500	4/500	4/500

Weaponry
Missile [Hull:F] +2.
Sandcaster [Hull:F] +2.

Equipment
Modules: Bunkroom, hardened Command Bridge, Computer Bay, Electronic Warfare, Engineering, Information Center, Probe Bay, Utility.

Statistics
Dim.: 21'×21'×42'	*Payload:* 10 tons	*Lwt.:* 170 tons
Volume: 30 dtons	*SizeMod:* +7	*Price:* MCr65.8

HP: 6,000

EXPANDABLE BASE (TL12)

An experimental project by the University of Regina, the expandable base is only usable dirtside. Upon deployment, the module unfolds and doubles in size, providing a comfortable base camp. Note that all areas of the module, including the hold, must be empty when the module is collapsed. It takes about 20 minutes to fully deploy the base, and an hour to collapse it.

The expandable-base module has no crew. It features a sealed body. Its modules cannot be utilized until the base is expanded on a planet's surface.

Subassemblies: SL Hull.
Occupancy: 14   **Cargo:** 4 dtons

Armor	F	RL	B	T	U
All:	4/500	4/500	4/500	4/500	4/500

Equipment

Modules: Basic Bridge, 2 Complete Workshops, 2 Lab, Sickbay, Small-craft Engineering, 2 Spacedock, 7 Staterooms, Utility.

Statistics

Dim.: 21′×21′×42′	*Payload:* 20 tons	*Lwt.:* 119 tons
Volume: 30 dtons	*SizeMod:* +7	*Price:* MCr6.3

HP: 6,000

FAST COURIER (TL12)

This module is used by the Navy for rapid physical transport between vessels in a squadron or fleet. Like the Marine's orbital-insertion module, the fast-courier module provides additional thrust, and thus cannot be used except in reinforced cutters (those with heavy or total compartmentalization). Space is provided for 12 passengers and a single senior officer in a stateroom/office.

The fast-courier module has no crew. It features heavy compartmentalization and a sealed body.

Subassemblies: SL Hull.

Occupancy: See above   **Cargo:** 8 dtons

Armor	F	RL	B	T	U
All:	4/1,000	4/1,000	4/1,000	4/1,000	4/1,000

Equipment

Modules: Engineering, 9 Maneuver, Passenger, Stateroom, Utility.

Statistics

Dim.: 21′×21′×42′	*Payload:* 40 tons	*Lwt.:* 176 tons
Volume: 30 dtons	*SizeMod:* +7	*Price:* MCr7.8

HP: 6,000

FIGHTER POD (TL10)

This simple module provides space for a single 10-ton fighter and its crew. The hold space is used for replacement parts and weapon stores. The fighter is released through the belly of the module, so it cannot be deployed when the module is on the ground.

The fighter-pod module has a crew of two, the fighter pilot and the crew chief. It features a sealed body.

Subassemblies: SL Hull.

Occupancy: 2   **Cargo:** 3 dtons

Armor	F	RL	B	T	U
All:	4/100	4/100	4/100	4/100	4/100

Equipment

Modules: Engineering, 2 Stateroom, Utility, Vehicle Bay (10-ton fighter).

Statistics

Dim.: 21′×21′×42′	*Payload:* 72 tons	*Lwt.:* 117 tons
Volume: 30 dtons	*SizeMod:* +7	*Price:* MCr1.4

HP: 6,000

FIREFIGHTING (TL10)

This module provides firefighting capability for the modular cutter, and can commonly be seen at Class III starports and above. It comprises a belly turret fitted with one to three extra-heavy water cannons, and a large (20-space) tank capable of holding 75,000 gallons of water or fire-extinguisher foam. The module is fitted with louvers so that it can be refilled by skimming a local body of water, which takes 30 seconds at 100 mph. This requires the pilot to make a skill roll at -2. The louvers can be reversed to allow the cutter to water-bomb a large fire so that, in a single pass, the cutter can drench an area 100 yards wide by 1 mile long.

The firefighting module has a crew of one gunner. It features a sealed body.

Subassemblies: SL Hull, Turret +5.

Occupancy: 1 RCS   **Cargo:** 25 dtons

Armor	F	RL	B	T	U
All:	4/100	4/100	4/100	4/100	4/100

Weaponry

XH Water Cannon [Tur:F] (75,000 gallons) +2.

Statistics

Dim.: 21′×21′×42′	*Payload:* 354 tons	*Lwt.:* 385 tons
Volume: 30 dtons	*SizeMod:* +7	*Price:* MCr1.27

HP: 6,000 [Hull]   1,200 [Tur]

FUEL SKIMMER (TL10)

With this module, the cutter becomes a fuel skimmer for a larger craft. The two fuel-processing modules can refine a total of 16 fuel modules per hour, or the entire load in 82.5 minutes.

The fuel-skimmer module has no crew. It has a sealed body.

Subassemblies: SL Hull.

Armor	F	RL	B	T	U
All:	4/100	4/100	4/100	4/100	4/100

Equipment

Modules: 22 Fuel, 2 Fuel Processor.

Statistics

Dim.: 21′×21′×42′	*Payload:* -	*Lwt.:* 55 tons
Volume: 30 dtons	*SizeMod:* +7	*Price:* MCr5.9

HP: 6,000

Advanced

See p. 46. LWt. becomes 113, Price MCr6.7.

Armored

See p. 46. Lwt. becomes 198, Price MCr10.1.

Stealth

See p. 46. Lwt. becomes becomes 77, Price MCr12.2.

GARAGE (ATV) (TL10)

This module provides space for a vehicle up to 3,500 cf in a spacious vehicle dock. To assist in the deployment of the carried craft, a single winch is provided. Care must be taken to ensure that the carried vehicle does not increase the loaded weight beyond the specifications of the parent cutter. The garage (ATV) module has no crew. It features a sealed body.

Subassemblies: SL Hull.
Cargo: 9 dtons

Armor	F	RL	B	T	U
All:	4/100	4/100	4/100	4/100	4/100

Equipment
Modules: 14 Spacedock, 1 Winch.

Statistics

Dim.: 21'×21'×42'	*Payload:* 80 tons	*Lwt.:* 118 tons
Volume: 30 dtons	*SizeMod:* +7	*Price:* MCr0.9

HP: 6,000

Advanced

See p. 46. LWt. becomes 176, Price MCr1.6.

Armored

See p. 46. Lwt. becomes 260, Price MCr5.1.

Stealth

See p. 46. Lwt. becomes becomes 140, Price MCr7.2.

HIGH-CAPACITY BERTHING (TL10)

This module provides extended sleeping and living quarters for up to 80 persons, although preferred capacity is 20 persons. Despite its cramped conditions and a lack of privacy, it is sometimes used for long-range in-system travel where the passengers cannot afford better accommodations. Likewise, some corporations use it to transport large numbers of workers on routes taking more than one day, and it is often used at construction sites and colonies as short-term housing until more permanent (and more spacious) facilities can be constructed. As part of a modular space station, it may be used to house the "menial labor" workers – or the station owners may simply decide to use it as "no-frills" living space. A less obvious use, but one which the designers had in mind, is to evacuate large numbers of people at one time. Since the module is completely self-contained, it could serve as an escape pod in an emergency.

The high-capacity berthing module has a crew of one engineer when operating without a cutter. It features a sealed body.

Subassemblies: SL Hull.
Occupancy: See above   **Cargo:** 4 dtons

Armor	F	RL	B	T	U
All:	4/100	4/100	4/100	4/100	4/100

Equipment
Modules: 5 Bunkrooms, Engineering, Utility.

Statistics

Dim.: 21'×21'×42'	*Payload:* 20 tons	*Lwt.:* 86 tons
Volume: 30 dtons	*SizeMod:* +7	*Price:* MCr1.54

HP: 6,000

HIGH-CAPACITY TROOP-BERTHING (TL10)

This module is designed to provide extended sleeping and living quarters for up to 48 troops and two officers, although preferred capacity is 12 troops and one officer. Despite having cramped conditions and a lack of privacy, it is sometimes used for long-range in-system travel where the troops cannot get a dedicated troop transport.

It also is used at invasion sites and wargame locations as short-term housing until more permanent (and more spacious) facilities can be constructed. As part of a modular space station, it may be used to house the protection force, or the government may simply decide to use these instead of better accommodation modules.

A gymnasium for up to four people is also provided, with an extra entrance via the deck iris valve aft. This prevents a steady stream of people past the officers' stateroom. All bunks on the upper level are double-stacked. The four on the lower level are single bunks, typically reserved for ranking NCOs.

The high-capacity troop-berthing module has a crew of one engineer when operating without a cutter. It features a sealed body.

Subassemblies: SL Hull.
Occupancy: See above   **Cargo:** 0.5 dtons

Armor	F	RL	B	T	U
All:	4/100	4/100	4/100	4/100	4/100

Equipment
Modules: 3 Armoury, 3 Bunkroom, Engineering, Gymnasium, Stateroom, Utility.

Statistics

Dim.: 21'×21'×42'	*Payload:* 2.5 tons	*Lwt.:* 80 tons
Volume: 30 dtons	*SizeMod:* +7	*Price:* MCr1.5

HP: 6,000

Laboratory (TL10)

This module provides lab facilities for a station or base, and can be deployed on a world's surface or in deep space. Staterooms are provided for three researchers (six can be accommodated with double occupancy). This module is often customized for specific types of research, and many custom variants exist.

The laboratory module has a crew of three to six scientific personnel. It features a sealed body.

Subassemblies: SL Hull.
Occupancy: 3-6   **Cargo:** 6 dtons

Armor	F	RL	B	T	U
All:	4/100	4/100	4/100	4/100	4/100

Equipment
Modules: Engineering, 2 Laboratory, 3 Stateroom, Utility.

Statistics
Dim.: 21'×21'×42'   *Payload:* 30 tons   *Lwt.:* 97 tons
Volume: 30 dtons   *SizeMod:* +7   *Price:* MCr3.4

HP: 6,000

Logistics (TL10)

With this module, a cutter can serve as a repair vessel, docking alongside a troubled ship and rendering aid. Two logistics bays provide maintenance and construction abilities, while a small cargo bay holds spare parts. A bunkroom is present for the work crew. It differs from the portable field shop in that it is not intended for long-term occupancy.

The logistics module has a crew of up to four mechanics. It features a sealed body and heavy compartmentalization.

Subassemblies: SL Hull.
Occupancy: 1-4   **Cargo:** 8 dtons

Armor	F	RL	B	T	U
All:	4/100	4/100	4/100	4/100	4/100

Equipment
Modules: Bunkroom, Engineering, 2 Logistics, Utility.

Statistics
Dim.: 21'×21'×42'   *Payload:* 40 tons   *Lwt.:* 145 tons
Volume: 30 dtons   *SizeMod:* +7   *Price:* MCr1.6

HP: 6,000

Lounge (TL10)

This module provides simple entertainment and relaxation. Gravity is provided. While some nobles use this module in lieu of a normal passenger module, it is more commonly found on stations or large merchant modular vessels.

The lounge module has no crew. It features a sealed body.

Subassemblies: SL Hull.
Occupancy: See above   **Cargo:** 2 dtons

Armor	F	RL	B	T	U
All:	4/100	4/100	4/100	4/100	4/100

Equipment
Modules: Engineering, 2 Large Room, Utility.

Statistics
Dim.: 21'×21'×42'   *Payload:* 10 tons   *Lwt.:* 50 tons
Volume: 30 dtons   *SizeMod:* +7   *Price:* MCr1.3

HP: 6,000

Low Berth (TL10)

This contains 176 low berths, and a sickbay to deal with hibernation emergencies. The low-berth module can be used in merchant ventures to carry passengers, or can be used in emergency situations as a lifeboat.

The low-berth module has no crew needs except the medics required for any frozen passengers. It features a sealed body.

Subassemblies: SL Hull.
Occupancy: See above

Armor	F	RL	B	T	U
All:	4/100	4/100	4/100	4/100	4/100

Equipment
Modules: 44 Low Berth, 2 Sickbay.

Statistics
Dim.: 21'×21'×42'   *Payload:* -   *Lwt.:* 114 tons
Volume: 30 dtons   *SizeMod:* +7   *Price:* MCr10.7

HP: 6,000

Luxury Passenger Transport (TL10)

A more sophisticated alternative to the standard passenger module, the luxury passenger module holds fewer people, but has a lounge and more room. Many of these modules are in use by nobles, who often spend a great deal of extra money to enhance the interior.

The luxury passenger-transport module has a crew of two stewards. It features a sealed body.

Subassemblies: SL Hull.
Occupancy: See above   **Cargo:** 10 dtons

Armor	F	RL	B	T	U
All:	4/100	4/100	4/100	4/100	4/100

Equipment
Modules: Engineering, Large Room 2 Passenger, Utility.

Statistics
Dim.: 21'×21'×42'   *Payload:* 50 tons   *Lwt.:* 91 tons
Volume: 30 dtons   *SizeMod:* +7   *Price:* MCr1.5

HP: 6,000

Luxury Quarters (TL10)

An expensive counterpart to the standard quarters module, the luxury quarters module can transport a single individual (or couple) in elegant style. A large suite is provided (two staterooms merged into one large one), as well as a parlor and receiving room. Like the luxury passenger module, this module is often customized further by its owner.

The luxury-quarters module needs no crew, though stewards are often provided. It features a sealed body.

Subassemblies: SL Hull.
Occupancy: See above   **Cargo:** 4 dtons

Armor	F	RL	B	T	U
All:	4/100	4/100	4/100	4/100	4/100

Equipment
Modules: Engineering, Large Room 2 Staterooms, Utility.

Statistics

Dim.: 21'×21'×42'	*Payload:* 20 tons	*Lwt.:* 65 tons
Volume: 30 dtons	*SizeMod:* +7	*Price:* MCr1.4

HP: 6,000

"Soldiers being what they are, the military modules rapidly acquired nicknames. The firebase module was known as the 'porta-coffin,' the command module 'brass in a can,' and the medevac module 'the bus.'"

– Captain Miles Hawthorne, **Aces and Eights: The History of the 1188th Lift Infantry**

Marine Command (TL12)

This module serves as headquarters for commanding and directing a Marine landing force, and is unavailable outside of the Imperial Marines. The Marine command module provides no room for personnel; a quarters or berthing module is usually assigned to be placed with it to provide living quarters. The command bridge, information center, and traffic-control centers can manage all communications assets up to the company level, as well as direct artillery strikes and ortillery bombardments. The two offices are available for command staff.

The Marine-command module has a crew of two communications specialists, two fire-direction controllers, two COACC controllers, four clerks, and appropriate command staff. It features a sealed body, total compartmentalization, basic stealth, and basic emission cloaking.

Subassemblies: SL Hull.
Occupancy: See above   **Cargo:** 0.5 dtons

Armor	F	RL	B	T	U
All:	4/2,000	4/2,000	4/2,000	4/2,000	4/2,000

Equipment
Modules: Hardened Command Bridge, Engineering, Information Center, 2 Offices, Traffic Control, Utility.

Statistics

Dim.: 21'×21'×42'	*Payload:* 2.5 tons	*Lwt.:* 278 tons
Volume: 30 dtons	*SizeMod:* +7	*Price:* MCr52.7

HP: 24,000

Marine Firebase (TL12)

This module is designed to be dropped planetside and serve as an Imperial Marine forward base. It is equipped to serve a single squad in cramped accommodations. The module contains a cockpit bridge for the communications and sensor equipment, bunkrooms for 12, a battledress morgue, two autodocs, and a vehicle bay for an *Astrin* APC. A single turret is present for base defense; it cannot be used when the module is being carried. The Firebase module is not available to the public.

This module has no crew. It features a sealed body, total compartmentalization, basic stealth, and basic emission cloaking.

Subassemblies: SL Hull, Turret +5.
Occupancy: See above

Armor	F	RL	B	T	U
All:	4/2,000	4/2,000	4/2,000	4/2,000	4/2,000

Weaponry
Fusion Gun [Tur:F] +2.
Missile Launcher [Tur:F] +2.

Equipment
Modules: Hardened Cockpit Bridge, Engineering, 3 Bunkroom, Information Center, Morgue, 4 Spacedock (for *Astrin*), Sickbay.

Statistics

Dim.: 21'×21'×42'	*Payload:* 12 tons	*Lwt.:* 280 tons
Volume: 30 dtons	*SizeMod:* +7	*Price:* MCr30.5

HP: 24,000 [Hull]   1,200 [Tur]

Medevac (TL10)

Unlike the medical module, the medevac is not intended to support a medical staff. It is simply designed to mass-evacuate wounded. The module can carry 36 lightly wounded/unwounded in passenger seats, 36 stable wounded on stretchers with emergency-support units, and 36 critical evacuees in automeds.

The medevac module needs no crew, though medics are often provided. It features a sealed body.

Subassemblies: SL Hull.
Occupancy: See above   **Cargo:** 1 dton

Armor	F	RL	B	T	U
All:	4/100	4/100	4/100	4/100	4/100

Equipment
Modules: Engineering, 3 Advanced Evacuation, 3 Basic Evacuation, 3 Passenger, Utility.

Statistics

Dim.: 21'×21'×42'	*Payload:* 62 tons	*Lwt.:* 67 tons
Volume: 30 dtons	*SizeMod:* +7	*Price:* MCr3.7

HP: 6,000

Medical (TL10)

This module provides medical facilities for a station or base, and can be deployed on a world's surface or in deep space. It can also be used as a portable emergency hospital for disaster relief, rescue operations, and so on.

The medical module has a crew of three medics. It features a sealed body.

Subassemblies: SL Hull.

Occupancy: See above   **Cargo:** 6 dtons

Armor	F	RL	B	T	U
All:	4/100	4/100	4/100	4/100	4/100

Equipment

Modules: Engineering, 4 Sickbay, 3 Stateroom, Utility.

Statistics

Dim.: 21′×21′×42′	*Payload:* 30 tons	*Lwt.:* 80 tons
Volume: 30 dtons	*SizeMod:* +7	*Price:* MCr2

HP: 6,000

Mining Pallet (TL10)

A non-jump capable version of the *Seeker*, the mining pallet is intended to ply asteroid belts for minerals and riches. With only two bunks, accommodations are very tight, but many prospectors prefer to operate alone. The turret mounts a laser for mining operations, and the lab is equipped to analyze rock samples.

The mining pallet has no crew needs. It features a sealed body.

Subassemblies: USL Hull, Turret +5.

Occupancy: See above   **Cargo:** 25 dtons

Armor	F	RL	B	T	U
All:	4/100	4/100	4/100	4/100	4/100

Weaponry

Laser [Tur:F] +2.

Equipment

Modules: Lab, Life Support, Small-Craft Bridge Add-on, Utility.

Statistics

Dim.: 21′×21′×42′	*Payload:* 125 tons	*Lwt.:* 184 tons
Volume: 30 dtons	*SizeMod:* +7	*Price:* MCr2.9

HP: 6,000 [Hull]   1,200 [Tur]

Nuclear Damper (TL12)

This module can provide tactical damper support, either on the move in escort duties, or on the ground with a base. Staterooms for the crew are provided.

The nuclear-damper module has a crew of one damper operator; up to three maintenance personnel may also be housed. It features a sealed body, total compartmentalization, basic stealth, and basic emission cloaking.

Subassemblies: SL Hull.

Occupancy: See above   **Cargo:** 2 dtons

Armor	F	RL	B	T	U
All:	4/100	4/100	4/100	4/100	4/100

Equipment

Modules: Hardened Cockpit Bridge, Information Center, 8 Nuclear Damper (25-mile range), 2 Stateroom, Utility.

Statistics

Dim.: 21′×21′×42′	*Payload:* 10 tons	*Lwt.:* 278 tons
Volume: 30 dtons	*SizeMod:* +7	*Price:* MCr40.4

HP: 24,000

Orbital Insertion (TL12)

This module is designed to drop four marine squads (36 men) from orbit. Plenty of capsule space is provided for decoys. This module is not intended for long-term occupation. The design is unusual – like the fast courier, the orbital-insertion module has thruster units to supplement the cutter's own drives. The exhaust ports slide out from the module after launch. Because of the additional flight stress, only cutters with heavy or total compartmentalization can take advantage of these maneuver drives. On any other vessel, the maneuver units are not used.

The orbital-insertion module has a crew of two jumpmasters. It features a sealed body, total compartmentalization, radical stealth, and radical emission cloaking.

Subassemblies: SL Hull.

Occupancy: See above   **Cargo:** 2 dtons

Armor	F	RL	B	T	U
All:	4/1,200	4/1,200	4/1,200	4/1,200	4/1,200

Equipment

Modules: 10 Capsule Launcher (20 tubes), 5 Capsule Rack (80 capsules), 4 Maneuver, 2 Morgue, 3 Passenger.

Statistics

Dim.: 21′×21′×42′	*Payload:* 120 tons	*Lwt.:* 435 tons
Volume: 30 dtons	*SizeMod:* +7	*Price:* MCr13.1

HP: 24,000

Passenger (TL10)

This module is not intended to be used separately from the hull, as it only provides life support for 24 hours or less. The main purpose of the module is the transport of passengers and cargo from ship to ship, ship to world surface, or the reverse.

The passenger module has a crew of one steward. It can carry 48 passengers and features a sealed body.

Subassemblies: SL Hull.

Occupancy: 49   **Cargo:** 19 dtons

Armor	F	RL	B	T	U
All:	4/100	4/100	4/100	4/100	4/100

Equipment

Modules: Engineering, 4 Passenger.

Statistics

Dim.: 21'×21'×42'   *Payload:* 95 tons   *Lwt.:* 125 tons
Volume: 30 dtons   *SizeMod:* +7   *Price:* MCr1.3

HP: 6,000

Advanced

See p. 46. LWt. becomes 183, Price MCr1.9.

Armored

See p. 46. Lwt. becomes 265, Price MCr3.5.

Stealth

See p. 46. Lwt. becomes 147, Price MCr7.4.

Planetary Infrastructure (TL10)

This module, fitting a standard modular cutter, is designed to provide a young colony with a thorough, if basic, set of planetary electronic systems. Towed into orbit and released, the module includes basic station-keeping thrusters, designed to allow the module to remain in orbit, and even maneuver slightly for an indefinite period of time. While in orbit, the module's extensive electronics provide the local population with communication and traffic-control capabilities. Additionally, the module carries spare anchor beacons, as well as spare GPS satellites. The module's thrusters allow sufficient mobility so that the GPS constellation can be maintained and re-seeded as long as spares hold out. The accommodations are rather sparse, and crews are rotated often to maintain health and happiness.

The planetary-infrastructure module has a crew of pilot/commander, engineer, communications officer, and four traffic controllers. It features a sealed body.

Subassemblies: USL Hull.

Occupancy: See above   **Cargo:** 2 dtons

Armor	F	RL	B	T	U
All:	4/100	4/100	4/100	4/100	4/100

Equipment

Modules: Basic Bridge, 3 Bunkroom, Engineering, Enhanced Communications, Maneuver, Office, Probe, Traffic Control, Utility.

Statistics

Dim.: 21'×21'×42'   *Payload:* 10 tons   *Lwt.:* 108 tons
Volume: 30 dtons   *SizeMod:* +7   *Price:* MCr21.5

HP: 6,000

Portable Field Shop (TL10)

This module is actually used more often on its own than attached to a cutter. Most often, it is used as part of better equipped Class I starports or temporary ground bases. In either case, it services all local vehicles and equipment, and, if required, starships. Also, the module is often used as part of long-term modular space stations, providing vital repair facilities.

The cargo bay has a large hatch on the port side of the module; it can't be accessed by ground vehicles unless the module is partially sunk into the ground. Its primary shortcoming is that the module can't work on very large components internally.

The portable field shop may be left attached to a cutter, providing a truly mobile repair facility. This usage is popular with militaries, governments, and megacorps.

The portable field-shop module has a crew of three to six technicians. It features a sealed body.

Subassemblies: SL Hull.

Occupancy: See above   **Cargo:** 5 dtons

Armor	F	RL	B	T	U
All:	4/100	4/100	4/100	4/100	4/100

Equipment

Modules: Engineering, Logistics, 3 Stateroom, Utility.

Statistics

Dim.: 21'×21'×42'   *Payload:* 25 tons   *Lwt.:* 102 tons
Volume: 30 dtons   *SizeMod:* +7   *Price:* MCr1.5

HP: 4,500

Prison Transport (TL10)

This module is designed for the transport of prisoners from different locales. Three levels of security are provided: normal passenger seating (with locking straps), three brigs, and eight cryotubes. An office serves as a security area, while a small hold serves as an armory. Two automeds are present in the case of an emergency.

The prison-transport module has a crew of security personnel as needed, plus a medic. It features a sealed body and total compartmentalization.

Subassemblies: SL Hull.

Occupancy: See above   **Cargo:** 2 dtons

Armor	F	RL	B	T	U
All:	4/100	4/100	4/100	4/100	4/100

Equipment

Modules: 3 Brig, Engineering, 2 Low Berth, Office, 2 Passenger, Sickbay, Utility.

Statistics

Dim.: 21′×21′×42′	*Payload:* 10 tons	*Lwt.:* 94 tons
Volume: 30 dtons	*SizeMod:* +7	*Price:* MCr2.3

HP: 6,000

QUARTERS (TL10)

This module is designed to provide shelter for a surface or deep-space station or base. At double occupancy, the module can support 10 inhabitants for an indefinite period of time (provided food and other perishables are occasionally replenished). Used with a cutter hull, it can provide long-duration sublight transport.

The quarters module requires no crew. It features a sealed body.

Subassemblies: SL Hull.

Occupancy: See above   **Cargo:** 2 dtons

Armor	F	RL	B	T	U
All:	4/100	4/100	4/100	4/100	4/100

Equipment

Modules: Engineering, 5 Stateroom, Utility.

Statistics

Dim.: 21′×21′×42′	*Payload:* 10 tons	*Lwt.:* 62 tons
Volume: 30 dtons	*SizeMod:* +7	*Price:* MCr1.4

HP: 6,000

Advanced

See p. 46. LWt. becomes 117, Price MCr1.9.

Armored

See p. 46. Lwt. becomes 202, Price MCr5.4.

Stealth

See p. 46. Lwt. becomes 82, Price MCr7.4.

RECOVERY (TL10)

This module is primarily for the recovery of damaged vehicles, although it also sees use as a flying crane for those situations where a conventional crane is not practical. The module is an open frame holding two winches, each capable of lifting 100 tons, and a duplicate control room adjoining the rear of the cutter's forward section, facing backward. A large clamp (two clamp modules) fixes the load so that it will not shift in flight. It is fitted with floodlights for night operations, though the military version also includes a 0.5-mile PESA.

The recovery module has a crew of one loadmaster.

Subassemblies: SL Hull.

Occupancy: 1

Equipment

Modules: 2 Clamp, Duplicate Control, 2 External Cradle, 2 Winch.

Statistics

Dim.: 21′×21′×42′	*Payload:* 200 tons	*Lwt.:* 254 tons
Volume: 30 dtons	*SizeMod:* +7	*Price:* MCr1.1

HP: 6,000

RECREATION (TL10)

Recreation modules come in many variants. These modules typically host the same sort of entertainment as seen in a USO show on old Terra. The module's cutter picks its way through the different outposts wherever troops may be in need of some rest, relaxation, and entertainment.

This particular variant, the Type A, has a large recreation facility for 100 people along with a four-person gymnasium and 1 dton of cargo, the latter two located on the lower level. In more permanent locations, such as a modular space station or a Class I/II, it may be used as the main lounge, a school, or cafeteria. The module has also found use as a temporary disaster-relief center, giving refugees hot meals and a place to try to locate loved ones. It is not self-contained and must be connected to a working power supply.

The recreation module requires no crew. It features a sealed body.

Subassemblies: SL Hull.

Occupancy: See above   **Cargo:** 1.5 dtons

Armor	F	RL	B	T	U
All:	4/100	4/100	4/100	4/100	4/100

Equipment

Modules: Gymnasium, 2 Large Room.

Statistics

Dim.: 21′×21′×42′	*Payload:* 7.5 tons	*Lwt.:* 32 tons
Volume: 30 dtons	*SizeMod:* +7	*Price:* MCr0.7

HP: 6,000

Safari (TL10)

Designed for safari trips, this module has no accommodations; it is intended to operate with a base camp or from onboard a vessel. Acceleration couches are provided for 12, and a large room serves as an observation deck and trophy room. Large shutters open the observation room to the exterior, to allow hunting. Animal transport includes a 6-ton cargo hold and a swimming pool for sea creatures. The pool can be drained if more dry storage is needed.

The safari module requires no crew. It features a sealed body and total compartmentalization.

Subassemblies: SL Hull.

Occupancy: See above   **Cargo:** 7 dtons

Armor	F	RL	B	T	U
All:	4/100	4/100	4/100	4/100	4/100

Equipment

Modules: Lounge, Passenger, Swimming Pool.

Statistics

Dim.: 21'×21'×42'   *Payload:* 61 tons   *Lwt.:* 87 tons
Volume: 30 dtons   *SizeMod:* +7   *Price:* MCr0.8

HP: 6,000

Scout Survey Base (TL10)

This is one of several custom-built modules for the IISS. It is intended to be left on a world with a small team to perform survey operations.

The Scout survey base module supports only four people – but the Mobile Exploration Base (from p. T:FI33) carried within it can support six, for a total of 10 team members. It features a sealed body.

Subassemblies: SL Hull.

Occupancy: See above

Armor	F	RL	B	T	U
All:	4/100	4/100	4/100	4/100	4/100

Equipment

Modules: Basic Bridge, Bunkroom, Lab, Probe Bay, Sickbay, Small-Craft Engineering, Survey, Utility, 8 Vehicle Bay (holds Mobile Exploration Base).

Statistics

Dim.: 21'×21'×42'   *Payload:* 22 tons   *Lwt.:* 95 tons
Volume: 30 dtons   *SizeMod:* +7   *Price:* MCr19.8

HP: 6,000

Scout Support Base (TL10)

This module serves as a miniature Scout way station. The SSB provides limited repair facilities, traffic control, an office, and storage space for parts. While there is a bunkroom to hold up to four Scouts, this module is often paired with a quarters module to make a proper base. If the base is situated near a body of water, often a couple of fuel-skimmer modules will be placed nearby to act as a fuel farm.

The Scout support base module supports four Scout personnel. It features a sealed body.

Subassemblies: SL Hull.

Occupancy: 1-4   **Cargo:** 5 dtons

Armor	F	RL	B	T	U
All:	4/100	4/100	4/100	4/100	4/100

Equipment

Modules: Bunkroom, Cockpit Bridge, 2 Complete Workshops, Office, Spacedock (holds up to 500 cf air/raft), Traffic Control.

Statistics

Dim.: 21'×21'×42'   *Payload:* 30 tons   *Lwt.:* 106 tons
Volume: 30 dtons   *SizeMod:* +7   *Price:* MCr16

HP: 6,000

> "When I was with the Survey Branch, I was assigned to a station studying a gaseous anomaly in the Ushkhir system. We finished the study, and I was to be transferred to another station, but the chief told me not to bother to pack – they were going to move the whole crew quarters pod on one of those jump cutters. I didn't even have to clean out the refrigerator . . ."
>
> – Karen Isoruku, IISS

Search and Rescue (TL10)

A design commissioned by the SPA, the SAR pod allows a cutter to act as a drive unit for another ship, by grappling itself to the stricken vessel. The ventral surface of the pod is taken up by the massive electromagnetic clamps, while the rest of the pod is made up of 16 low berths and extra thruster units. Due to the stresses this module can generate, it can only be used on vessels with heavy or total compartmentalization.

The search and rescue module has no crew. It features a sealed body.

Subassemblies: SL Hull.

Armor	F	RL	B	T	U
All:	4/100	4/100	4/100	4/100	4/100

Equipment

Modules: 18 External Grapple, 4 Low Berth, 4 Manuever.

Statistics

Dim.: 21′×21′×42′   *Payload:* -   *Lwt.:* 331 tons
Volume: 30 dtons   *SizeMod:* +7   *Price:* MCr9.4
HP: 6,000

Sensor (TL12)

The sensor pod allows a cutter to operate as a remote detection picket. Cutters so fitted can use active sensors while not exposing the fleet to detection. This module has only recently become available to a select number of universities, who are altering it for scientific use. All other such modules are in use by the Imperial Navy.

The sensor module has a crew of four sensor operators, one each for the active EM and passive EM suites, a probes operator, and an analyst. It features a sealed body, total compartmentalization, radical stealth, and radical emission cloaking.

Subassemblies: SL Hull.
Occupancy: 4 RCS

Armor	F	RL	B	T	U
All:	4/1,000	4/1,000	4/1,000	4/1,000	4/1,000

Equipment

Modules: Advanced Sensors, Bunkroom, hardened Command Bridge, Computer Bay, Information Center, Life Support, Probe Bay, Small-Craft Engineering, Utility.

Statistics

Dim.: 21′×21′×42′   *Payload:* -   *Lwt.:* 203 tons
Volume: 30 dtons   *SizeMod:* +7   *Price:* MCr89.1
HP: 6,000

Small Craft Bay (TL10)

The small-craft bay cutter module can carry a pair of 10-dton small craft, usually 10-ton launches. It is primarily used with modular space stations to provide them with auxiliary-craft needs. It also has some use as a vehicle garage with ground bases. There are several variants on the basic design. One replaces the two bays with one capable of holding a more useful 20-ton gig (the module's loaded weight becomes 125 standard tons). Another variant, moderately common on space stations, replaces the two launches with lifeboats (the module's weight again becomes 125 tons). A much rarer variant carries two *Iramda* 10-ton fighters.

The module's primary weaknesses are the limited size of vessels that can be carried and the fact that another cutter module must hold the crews of the carried craft for anything more than very short-term operations.

The small-craft bay module has no crew. It features a sealed body.

Subassemblies: SL Hull.
Cargo: 2 dtons

Armor	F	RL	B	T	U
All:	4/100	4/100	4/100	4/100	4/100

Equipment

Modules: 2 11-ton Vehicle Bays (see above for specific 10-ton craft held).

Statistics

Dim.: 21′×21′×42′   *Payload:* 84 tons   *Lwt.:* 109 tons
Volume: 30 dtons   *SizeMod:* +7   *Price:* MCr0.7
HP: 6,000

Standard Commercial (TL10)

Commonly used by large liners, the standard commercial module is a jack of all trades and master of none. It provides all the necessary services such a vessel would need – transport of passengers, low berths, and cargo. A collapsible fuel tank that expands into the cargo bay and a fuel processor also allow this module to refuel unstreamlined ships, if necessary. Gravity is provided. Capacity is 48 passengers, 32 low berths, and 10 dtons of cargo or fuel.

The standard commercial module requires a steward if passengers are carried; otherwise, it has no crew. It features a sealed body.

Subassemblies: SL Hull.
Occupancy: See above   **Cargo:** 12 dtons

Armor	F	RL	B	T	U
All:	4/100	4/100	4/100	4/100	4/100

Equipment

Modules: Collapsible Fuel Tank, Engineering, Fuel Processor, 8 Low Berth, 4 Passenger, Utility.

Statistics

Dim.: 21′×21′×42′   *Payload:* 60 tons   *Lwt.:* 129 tons
Volume: 30 dtons   *SizeMod:* +7   *Price:* MCr4.7
HP: 6,000

Survey (TL10)

A simple design in use by both the IISS and universities, the survey module is intended to be placed in orbit to map and detail a world. It has a crew of three survey-team members. It features a sealed body.

Subassemblies: SL Hull.
Occupancy: 3-6

Armor	F	RL	B	T	U
All:	4/100	4/100	4/100	4/100	4/100

Equipment

Modules: Engineering, Office, Probe Bay, 3 Stateroom, Survey, Utility.

Statistics

Dim.: 21′×21′×42′   *Payload:* -   *Lwt.:* 60 tons
Volume: 30 dtons   *SizeMod:* +7   *Price:* MCr16.4
HP: 6,000

THEATER (TL10)

The theater module contains a holoprojector and seating for 100. It can serve as a portable classroom, briefing room, or even as a "town hall" for a colony settlement. The holoprojector can be stowed under the floor, and a 27'-by-18' side hatch is included for joining the module with the traveling stage module (see below). The module is internally powered, and a full airlock and life support is also included.

The theater module has no crew. It features a sealed body.

Subassemblies: SL Hull.
Occupancy: 100 RS   **Cargo:** 2 dtons

Armor	F	RL	B	T	U
All:	4/100	4/100	4/100	4/100	4/100

Equipment
Modules: Engineering, Theater, Utility.

Statistics
Dim.: 21'×21'×42'	*Payload:* 10 tons	*Lwt.:* 52 tons
Volume: 30 dtons	*SizeMod:* +7	*Price:* MCr1.4

HP: 6,000

TRAVELING STAGE (TL10)

Often used by established traveling theater troupes or bands, the traveling-stage module contains all of the basics for an open-air performance. The stateroom space is divided into two common dressing rooms, and the cargo space is used for storing props, instruments, etc. A 27'-by-18' side hatch exposes the stage. Internal power allows for the module to be left at a venue and retrieved at the end of a performance run. For use in hostile environment or when formal seating is required, the module can be coupled with the theater module (see above).

The traveling-stage module has no crew. It features a sealed body.

Subassemblies: SL Hull.
Occupancy: See above   **Cargo:** 2 dtons

Armor	F	RL	B	T	U
All:	4/100	4/100	4/100	4/100	4/100

Equipment
Modules: Engineering, Stage, Stateroom, Utility.

Statistics
Dim.: 21'×21'×42'	*Payload:* 10 tons	*Lwt.:* 52 tons
Volume: 30 dtons	*SizeMod:* +7	*Price:* MCr1.4

HP: 6,000

TROOP TRANSPORT (TL10)

This is a simple module for the transport of troops and their equipment. Up to 48 soldiers, along with support vehicles, can be carried.

The troop-transport module has no crew. It features a sealed body. The listed loaded weight does not include the weight of any vehicles (or cargo) carried in the spacedock.

Subassemblies: SL Hull.
Occupancy: 48 RS   **Cargo:** 6 dtons

Armor	F	RL	B	T	U
All:	4/500	4/500	4/500	4/500	4/500

Equipment
Modules: 4 Passenger, 14 Spacedock (holds any 3,500 cf of vehicles).

Statistics
Dim.: 21'×21'×42'	*Payload:* 30 tons	*Lwt.:* 137 tons
Volume: 30 dtons	*SizeMod:* +7	*Price:* MCr2

HP: 6,000

TUGBOAT CUTTER (TL10)

The tugboat-cutter module is common around orbital and planetary shipyards, as well as many starports. In effect, it turns a cutter into a "space towtruck," capable of hauling disabled or unpowered shipping. The module can handle up to 2,687.5 standard tons, which covers most civilian shipping under 1,000 dtons. A slightly less common use is in construction, where the cutter/module tandem serves as a high-tech crane and transporter.

The cargo hold is used to carry various tools and cables that would be of use in recovering a disabled ship, as well as external landing lights to clamp on carried loads. Unlike most other cutter modules, the tugboat cutter module is fairly useless on its own, although it can (and has) been used as a portable "hardpoint" for non-cutters.

The tugboat-cutter module has a crew of one loadmaster, who works from the cutter, not the module. It features a sealed body.

Subassemblies: SL Hull.
Occupancy: See above   **Cargo:** 2.5 dtons

Armor	F	RL	B	T	U
All:	4/100	4/100	4/100	4/100	4/100

Equipment
Modules: 21.5 External Cradles.

Statistics
Dim.: 21'×21'×42'	*Payload:* 12.5 tons	*Lwt.:* 299 tons
Volume: 30 dtons	*SizeMod:* +7	*Price:* MCr1.9

HP: 6,000

VEHICLE TRANSPORT (TL10)

This module is a small spacedock capable of holding up to 12 dtons of vehicles. The particular variant illustrated on p. 114 includes a small fleet of air/rafts for expeditions or use as a simple "motor pool." There is a lift located near the spacedock doors to facilitate the movement of vehicles between decks. This model has stackable pallets allowing maximum use of volume.

Attached to a cutter, the module serves as a basic cargo hauler customized for vehicles. Used by itself, it makes a good enclosed hangar bay to keep vehicles out of the weather. It can also be used attached to a modular starport. Small hangar bays, strategically located around a starport, help to relieve the traffic load around a large bay.

The vehicle-transport module requires flight crews depending on its load. It features a sealed body. The listed loaded weight is for the illustrated "air/raft garage."

Subassemblies: SL Hull.
Occupancy: See above **Cargo:** 2.5 dtons

Armor	F	RL	B	T	U
All:	4/100	4/100	4/100	4/100	4/100

Equipment
Modules: 24 Spacedock (any 6,000 cf or 12 dtons of vehicles).

Statistics
Dim.: 21'×21'×42' *Payload:* 17 tons *Lwt.:* 65 tons
Volume: 30 dtons *SizeMod:* +7 *Price:* MCr0.8
HP: 6,000

WEAPONRY MODULES

A great number of modules have been designed to give offensive capabilities to the modular cutter. Detailed below are various models equipped with typical weaponry loads. Each module is self-powered, provides gravity and accommodations, and has a hold for repair parts or munitions. Thus, the modules can also be used as orbital weapons platforms or station weapon pods. Note that the firing arc of these modules is usually limited, as the turret usually extends out from a side or the belly. Models with belly guns cannot be deployed on ground bases.

Weapon Pod – Laser (TL10)

The weapon pod – laser module requires a crew of one gunner. It features a sealed body.

Subassemblies: SL Hull, Turret +5.
Occupancy: 1-2 **Cargo:** 16 dtons

Armor	F	RL	B	T	U
All:	4/100	4/100	4/100	4/100	4/100

Weaponry
3×Lasers [Tur:F] +2.

Equipment
Modules: Cockpit Bridge, Engineering, Stateroom, Utility.

Statistics
Dim.: 21'×21'×42' *Payload:* 80 tons *Lwt.:* 154 tons
Volume: 30 dtons *SizeMod:* +7 *Price:* MCr6.4
HP: 6,000 [Hull] 1,200 [Tur]

Advanced
See p. 46. LWt. becomes 209, Price MCr6.3.

Weapon Pod – Energy (TL10)

The weapon pod – energy module requires a crew of one gunner. It features a sealed body.

Subassemblies: SL Hull, Turret +5.
Occupancy: 1-2 **Cargo:** 16 dtons

Armor	F	RL	B	T	U
All:	4/100	4/100	4/100	4/100	4/100

Weaponry
2×Plasma [Tur:F] +2.

Equipment
Modules: Cockpit Bridge, Engineering, Stateroom, Utility.

Statistics
Dim.: 21'×21'×42' *Payload:* 80 tons *Lwt.:* 161 tons
Volume: 30 dtons *SizeMod:* +7 *Price:* MCr18.8
HP: 6,000 [Hull] 1,200 [Tur]

Advanced
See p. 46 and replace plasma with fusion weapons. LWt. becomes 213, Price MCr47.4.

Armored
See p. 46 and replace plasma with fusion weapons. Lwt. becomes 298, Price MCr50.9.

Weapon Pod – Missile (TL10)

The weapon pod – energy module requires a crew of one gunner. It features a sealed body.

Subassemblies: SL Hull, Turret +5.
Occupancy: 1-2 **Cargo:** 16 dtons

Armor	F	RL	B	T	U
All:	4/100	4/100	4/100	4/100	4/100

Weaponry
3×Missiles [Tur:F] +2.

Equipment
Modules: Cockpit Bridge, Engineering, Stateroom, Utility.

Statistics
Dim.: 21'×21'×42' *Payload:* 80 tons *Lwt.:* 153 tons
Volume: 30 dtons *SizeMod:* +7 *Price:* MCr3.5
HP: 6,000 [Hull] 1,200 [Tur]

Advanced
See p. 46. LWt. becomes 225, Price MCr4.3.

Armored
See p. 46. Lwt. becomes 310, Price MCr7.8.

Weapon Pod – Sand (TL10)

The weapon pod – sand module requires a crew of one gunner. It features a sealed body.

Subassemblies: SL Hull, Turret +5.
Occupancy: 1-2   **Cargo:** 16 dtons

Armor	F	RL	B	T	U
All:	4/100	4/100	4/100	4/100	4/100

Weaponry
3×Sandcasters [Tur:F] +2.

Equipment
Modules: Cockpit Bridge, Engineering, Stateroom, Utility.

Statistics

Dim.: 21'×21'×42'	*Payload:* 80 tons	*Lwt.:* 144 tons
Volume: 30 dtons	*SizeMod:* +7	*Price:* MCr4.7
HP: 6,000 [Hull]	1,200 [Tur]	

Advanced
See p. 46. LWt. becomes 201, Price MCr5.

STATION MODULES

These modules are designed to be deployed as segments of a larger facility. They are of limited use in modular shipping operations, though they could be pressed into such service. Note that any modular station or base is likely to also make use of several of the modules listed above that are intended primarily for shipping.

COMMAND (TL10)

This module provides the sensors and command equipment to control and monitor a station. Although the module has its own life support for emergency situations, it has no accommodations.

The command module requires a crew of two communications specialists. It features a sealed body.

Subassemblies: SL Hull.
Occupancy: 10 RCS   **Cargo:** 1 dton

Armor	F	RL	B	T	U
All:	4/100	4/100	4/100	4/100	4/100

Equipment
Modules: Command Bridge, Engineering, 4 Office, Utility.

Statistics

Dim.: 21'×21'×42'	*Payload:* 5 tons	*Lwt.:* 80 tons
Volume: 30 dtons	*SizeMod:* +7	*Price:* MCr11
HP: 6,000		

XBOAT RELAY (TL10)

A module in use by the IISS, the Naasirka IQR-34 functions as an in-system relay station for the Xboat network. The two communications officers use the massive commo system and computer network to handle the various dispatches sent and received. The IQR-34 is a dirtside module, and possesses no Utility component – its orbital counterpart is the IQR-44, which exchanges a dton of cargo for the necessary gravity systems.

The Xboat-relay module requires a crew of two communications specialists. It features a sealed body and total compartmentalization.

Subassemblies: SL Hull.
Occupancy: 2-4   **Cargo:** 2 dtons

Armor	F	RL	B	T	U
All:	4/100	4/100	4/100	4/100	4/100

Equipment
Modules: Cockpit Bridge, Engineering, 2 Stateroom, Xboat Relay.

Statistics

Dim.: 21'×21'×42'	*Payload:* 10 tons	*Lwt.:* 186 tons
Volume: 30 dtons	*SizeMod:* +7	*Price:* MCr7.4
HP: 6,000		

COMMERCIAL (TL10)

This simple pod provides space for offices and shops. It is highly customizable through the use of moveable partition and panels.

The commercial module requires no "basic" crew, but usually will have house operations for several office workers. It features a sealed body.

Subassemblies: SL Hull.
Occupancy: See above

Armor	F	RL	B	T	U
All:	4/100	4/100	4/100	4/100	4/100

Equipment
Modules: Engineering, Large Room, 3 Office, Utility.

Statistics

Dim.: 21'×21'×42'	*Payload:* -	*Lwt.:* 50 tons
Volume: 30 dtons	*SizeMod:* +7	*Price:* MCr1.4
HP: 6,000		

COMMUNICATIONS (TL10)

Designed to provide additional communications equipment to supplement the command pod, this module usually is found only on larger stations.

The communications module requires a crew of six commo specialists. It features a sealed body.

Subassemblies: SL Hull.

Occupancy: 10 RCS   **Cargo:** 1.5 dtons

Armor	F	RL	B	T	U
All:	4/100	4/100	4/100	4/100	4/100

Equipment

Modules: Command Bridge, Office, Small-Craft Engineering, Utility, Xboat Relay.

Statistics

Dim.: 21′×21′×42′	*Payload:* 7.5 tons	*Lwt.:* 208 tons
Volume: 30 dtons	*SizeMod:* +7	*Price:* MCr14.8

HP: 6,000

"It can be a little disconcerting to climb into the engineering module – the gravity twists 90 degrees just inside the door. A favorite trick engineers like to play on newbies is to ask them to carry something heavy out the door – my back hasn't been the same since."

– Kim Janoz-Humulka,
Twenty Years Aft of Center

ENGINEERING (TL10)

This module is interesting in that its gravity is oriented so that the end caps of the module are in the gravity plane. The pod is filled with two power plants and the shops necessary to maintain them.

The engineering module requires a crew of four engineers and four mechanics. It features a sealed body.

Subassemblies: SL Hull.

Occupancy: 5 RCS

Armor	F	RL	B	T	U
All:	4/100	4/100	4/100	4/100	4/100

Equipment

Modules: Basic Bridge, 2 Engineering, Fuel Processor, 2 Logistics, Office, 3.5 Power Module, Utility.

Statistics

Dim.: 21′×21′×42′	*Payload:* -	*Lwt.:* 121 tons
Volume: 30 dtons	*SizeMod:* +7	*Price:* MCr10.3

HP: 6,000

HYDROPONICS (TL10)

This body provides hydroponic food and life support for up to 400 people. The sides of the pod are transparent, to admit direct sunlight for the plant life, but the panels are polarized to allow adjustment of the light level.

Some stations also use these modules as parks and gardens – a little greenery is a great morale booster on an otherwise sterile station. The food output is sufficient for only 100 people in this case.

The hydroponics module requires a crew of two to four gardeners. It features a sealed body.

Subassemblies: SL Hull.

Occupancy: 2-4

Armor	F	RL	B	T	U
All:	4/100	4/100	4/100	4/100	4/100

Equipment

Modules: Engineering, Laboratory, Office, 16 Total Life Support.

Statistics

Dim.: 21′×21′×42′	*Payload:* -	*Lwt.:* 133 tons
Volume: 30 dtons	*SizeMod:* +7	*Price:* MCr2.8

HP: 6,000

"The station's garden was one of my favorite places when I was growing up. There's no night on a station, but there's a sleep/wake cycle, and they dim the lights in the quarters sections so people can sleep, but they kept the lights on most of the time in the six hydroponics modules they used as a garden. They grew fresh veggies and fruits in most of them, but the station commander reserved a small section of one pod for flowers – I guess for some people fresh flowers are as important as tomatoes and fresh basil."

– Helena Twelve-Trees
Faculty Brat

INDUSTRIAL (TL10)

This pod provides minimal construction and manufacturing capability to a station. These modules are often custom-built to service a particular industry.

The industrial module has widely varying crew needs. It features a sealed body.

Subassemblies: SL Hull.

Occupancy: See above   **Cargo:** 2 dtons

Armor	F	RL	B	T	U
All:	4/100	4/100	4/100	4/100	4/100

Equipment

Modules: Engineering, Laboratory, 3 Logistics, Office.

Statistics

Dim.: 21′×21′×42′	*Payload:* 10 tons	*Lwt.:* 142 tons
Volume: 30 dtons	*SizeMod:* +7	*Price:* MCr2.4

HP: 6,000

Traffic Control (TL10)

Useful for modular highports, the traffic-control module can provide flight-control services for a small planet. The offices are used as conference rooms and break rooms.

The traffic-control module has a crew of up to 16 flight-control officers. It features a sealed body.

Subassemblies: SL Hull.
Occupancy: 1-16   **Cargo:** 1 dton

Armor	F	RL	B	T	U
All:	4/100	4/100	4/100	4/100	4/100

Equipment
Modules: Command Bridge, Engineering, 2 Office, 2 Traffic Control, Utility.

Statistics

Dim.: 21′×21′×42′	*Payload:* 5 tons	*Lwt.:* 87 tons
Volume: 30 dtons	*SizeMod:* +7	*Price:* MCr36.3

HP: 6,000

Unusual Modules

Some modules are individual in nature – only a few copies exist. Others are designed with specific uses in mind; two examples follow.

MagLev Module (TL9)

This module is a simple streamlined cargo module that can travel along maglev train rails as well as be carried by a modular cutter. This makes it extremely useful to worlds with a maglev transport infrastructure, as the modules can be moved from the cutter directly to the rail, and then distributed across the planet.

The maglev module can also be launched into space by massdriver rails, thus providing cheap surface-to-orbit transit as long as only durable goods are carried. While the basic maglev module is used for cargo, other fittings are possible. On a magnetic rail, in vacuum, it can travel at 4 Gs empty or 1.1 Gs fully loaded.

The maglev module has no crew of its own. It features a sealed body.

Subassemblies: SL Hull.
Cargo: 20 dtons

Armor	F	RL	B	T	U
All:	4/100	4/100	4/100	4/100	4/100

Equipment
Modules: 4 MagLev.

Hiver Modules

These roughly rectangular, 25-dton containers can be found with increasing frequency in Imperial space as one approaches the Federation border.

Hiver Cargo (TL12)

The Hiver cargo module differs from the Imperial version by having Engineering and Utility components. Thus, the module can be used for a variety of other purposes. Imperial shipping concerns criticize the cost-ineffectiveness of such a design, but the Federation's economic system is different from the Imperium's, and the design has been fairly successful within Hiver borders.

The Hiver cargo module has no crew of its own. It features a sealed body.

Statistics

Dim.: 21′×21′×42′	*Payload:* 100 tons	*Lwt.:* 140 tons
Volume: 30 dtons	*SizeMod:* +7	*Price:* MCr4

HP: 6,000

Noble Transport (TL12)

Designed to serve a member of the nobility, this type of module provides luxurious accommodations, a private office, an information center, spartan quarters for two aides, and a sickbay. Each pod is luxuriously furnished, with MCr4 of interior fittings custom-built to the taste of each owner.

The noble-transport module has no crew of its own. It features a sealed body.

Subassemblies: SL Hull.
Occupancy: 3   **Cargo:** 1 dton

Armor	F	RL	B	T	U
All:	4/100	4/100	4/100	4/100	4/100

Equipment
Modules: Engineering, Information Center, Office, Sickbay, 3 Stateroom (1 double-sized and 2 half-sized), Utility.

Statistics

Dim.: 21′×21′×42′	*Payload:* 5 tons	*Lwt.:* 42 tons
Volume: 30 dtons	*SizeMod:* +7	*Price:* MCr8

HP: 6,000

Subassemblies: SL Hull.
Cargo: 18 dtons

Armor	F	RL	B	T	U
All:	4/700	4/700	4/700	4/700	4/700

Equipment
Modules: Engineering, Utility.

Statistics

Dim.: 18′×18′×60′	*Payload:* 90 tons	*Lwt.:* 156 tons
Volume: 25 dtons	*SizeMod:* +7	*Price:* MCr1.4

HP: 5,250

Hiver Embassy (TL12)

A deployable version of a small embassy (see *GURPS Traveller Alien Races 3*), this module provides living quarters for four (in double occupancy) and office space, as well as a communications suite and garage for an air/raft.

In addition to the usual internal duties of an embassy, these modules are often left on worlds that are being approached for membership in the Federation, or on foreign worlds as a point of contact to the Federation government.

The Hiver embassy module features a sealed body.

Subassemblies: SL Hull.
Occupancy: 1-4

Armor	F	RL	B	T	U
All:	4/700	4/700	4/700	4/700	4/700

Equipment
Modules: Engineering, Enhanced Communications, 2 Office, 1 Spacedock (holds up to 250 cf of any vehicle), 2 Stateroom, Utility.

Statistics
Dim.: 18'×18'×60'	*Payload:* 5 tons	*Lwt.:* 96 tons
Volume: 25 dtons	*SizeMod:* +7	*Price:* MCr2.1

HP: 5,250

Hiver Passenger (TL12)

The Hiver equivalent of the Imperial passenger module, these accommodations are slightly more comfortable, due to the presence of a Utility component for gravity. The Hiver model holds more passengers (72 people) at the expense of cargo space. Note that Hiver passenger areas are highly configurable, as the various member races of the Federation require different seating arrangements. For a given flight, the actual number of individuals carried can range from 20 to 120 sophonts.

The Hiver passenger module requires a steward during most operations. It features a sealed body.

Subassemblies: SL Hull.
Occupancy: See above   **Cargo:** 12 dtons

Armor	F	RL	B	T	U
All:	4/700	4/700	4/700	4/700	4/700

Equipment
Modules: Engineering, 6 Passenger, Utility.

Statistics
Dim.: 18'×18'×60'	*Payload:* 60 tons	*Lwt.:* 129 tons
Volume: 25 dtons	*SizeMod:* +7	*Price:* MCr1.9

HP: 5,250

Hiver War (TL12)

The basic Hiver war module is designed to meet any military need that a Hiver expedition might have. Seating for 12 Ithklur Marines and their gear, along with boarding equipment and capsule launchers, allows for small-unit invasions of ground

installations or enemy spacecraft. The spacedock is designed to carry either an APC for the Marines or a collection of warbots. This module is illegal in the Imperium.

The Hiver war module requires one gunner and one ECM specialist. It features a sealed body, total compartmentalization, basic stealth, and basic emission cloaking.

Subassemblies: SL Hull.
Occupancy: 5 RCS, 12 RS

Armor	F	RL	B	T	U
All:	4/700	4/700	4/700	4/700	4/700

Weaponry
Missile Launcher [Hull:B] +2.
Sandcaster [Hull:B] +2.

Equipment
Modules: Hardened Basic Bridge, Boarding Clamp, Capsule Launcher, Capsule Rack, Engineering, Hull Cutter, Jammer, Morgue, Passenger, Sickbay, 1 Spacedock (up to 250 cf of any vehicle or warbots), Utility.

Statistics
Dim.: 18'×18'×60'	*Payload:* 139 tons	*Lwt.:* 176 tons
Volume: 25 dtons	*SizeMod:* +7	*Price:* MCr23.1

HP: 5,250

MODULAR FRAME MODULES

The following modules are designed specifically for the K-series modular frames (p. 33). Each module is an unstreamlined, DR 100 hull with an appropriate power-plant component. Note that the K series can use any module not exceeding 250 standard tons, as long as the module is self-contained (that is, it either provides or does not require its own power and life support).

BRIDGE MODULES

These modules provide a standard bridge, staterooms, and cargo holds.

Displacement	Staterooms	Cargo	Mass	Cost	Crew
10	1	3	16	3.3	1-2
20	4	1	24	3.4	1-2
30	6	3	31	3.5	1-2

MANEUVER DRIVES

Available in three sizes, the maneuver-drive module provides thrust for the modular frame. Each frame is rated for the number of drive modules it can mount; this number does not take into account the size of the mounted drive modules.

Type	Displacement	Mass	Cost	Thrust	HP
Light	10	42	6.1	900	3,000
Medium	20	85	12.6	1,900	4,500
Heavy	30	127	19.2	2,900	6,000

For every 100 tons of drive modules installed, a single engineer is required.

MIXED DRIVE MODULE

This module provides both thrust and jump capability, but it cannot be combined with other mixed modules or jump modules to provide larger jump capability. This module counts as a drive module when checking drive-module limits.

Displacement	Mass	Cost	Jump Units	Thrust
30	100	26.3	5	1,400

JUMP MODULES

These modules provide jump drives and fuel. Note that jump performance will have to be calculated based on the size of the frame on which the jump module is installed. Only one jump module can be used at a time.

These modules do not count as drive modules. Note that ships may require more fuel in other modules. Since jump modules are very expensive, and often over- or underpowered, many owners of modular-frame ships forgo jump modules entirely and use their vessels as intrasystem craft.

All jump modules have 6,000 hit points.

Type	Jump Units	Fuel	Mass	Cost	Crew
Light	5	24	63	19.4	0-1
Medium	10	19	76	33.9	0-1
Heavy	20	9	103	62.8	1
Super-Heavy	29	0	127	88.8	1

JUMP SHIP MODULES

These 1,000-dton modules are designed to be carried by the *Kodriik*-class jump ship; see p. 34. Each module possesses clamps to attach another jump pod behind itself, thus forming a module train behind the *Kodriik*. Each module is also capable of operating independently, as an in-system spacecraft.

CARGO (TL12)

This simple module is dominated by its seven 100-dton holds.

The jump-ship cargo module requires a crew of four (captain/pilot, navigator, and two engineers) when operating independently. It features a sealed body.

Subassemblies: SL Hull.
Power & Propulsion: 34 Maneuver.
Occupancy: 4   **Cargo:** 700 dtons

Armor	F	RL	B	T	U
All:	4/100	4/100	4/100	4/100	4/100

Equipment
Modules: Basic Bridge, Engineering, 52 External Grapple, Life Support, 2 Stateroom, 2 Utility.

Statistics
Dim.: 50′×50′×200′   *Payload:* 3,500 tons   *Lwt.:* 4,437 tons
Volume: 1,000 dtons   *SizeMod:* +10   *Price:* MCr45.4
HP: 67,500
sAccel: 0.7 Gs/3.6 Gs empty   *aSpeed:* 2,591

LOW BERTH (TL12)

Commonly called the "icicle box," this module can carry 5,568 passengers in low berths. This pod is often used for colony seeding or evacuating. No facilities are present for awakening the passengers – they must be transferred off the ship first.

The jump-ship low berth module requires a crew of four (captain/pilot, navigator, and two engineers) when operating independently. It features a sealed body.

Subassemblies: SL Hull.
Power & Propulsion: 38 Maneuver.
Occupancy: 5,572

Armor	F	RL	B	T	U
All:	4/100	4/100	4/100	4/100	4/100

Equipment

Modules: Basic Bridge, Engineering, 52 External Grapple, 1,392 Low Berth, Life Support, 2 Stateroom, 2 Utility.

Statistics

Dim.: 50′×50′×200′ *Payload:* - *Lwt.:* 3,737 tons
Volume: 1,000 dtons *SizeMod:* +10 *Price:* MCr354.2

HP: 67,500

sAccel: 1 G *aSpeed:* 2,746

PASSENGER (TL12)

Two models of the passenger module are available. The first is the basic module, which is capable of transporting 120 (240 in double occupancy) passengers in relative comfort. The second version is a luxury model, which can carry 90 passengers (30 in double-sized suites, 60 in normal rooms) in very nice accommodations. In both cases, 20 staterooms are reserved for the command and service crew. The module provides a great deal of entertainment for its passengers, and many passenger modules operate as inter-system liners without ever hitching to a jump ship.

The jump-ship passenger module requires a crew of 20 (captain/pilot, navigator, commo operator, sensors operator, two engineers, two medics, 12 stewards) when operating independently. It features a sealed body.

Subassemblies: SL Hull.

Power & Propulsion: 22 Maneuver.

Occupancy: See above **Cargo:** 100 dtons

Armor	F	RL	B	T	U
All:	4/100	4/100	4/100	4/100	4/100

Equipment

Modules: Basic Bridge, Engineering, 52 External Grapple, Large Room, 8 Sickbay, Stage, 140 Stateroom, Swimming Pool, Theater, 2 Utility.

Statistics

Dim.: 50′×50′×200′ *Payload:* 525 tons *Lwt.:* 1,701 tons
Volume: 1,000 dtons *SizeMod:* +10 *Price:* MCr41

HP: 67,500

sAccel: 1.2 Gs/1.8 Gs empty *aSpeed:* 2,089

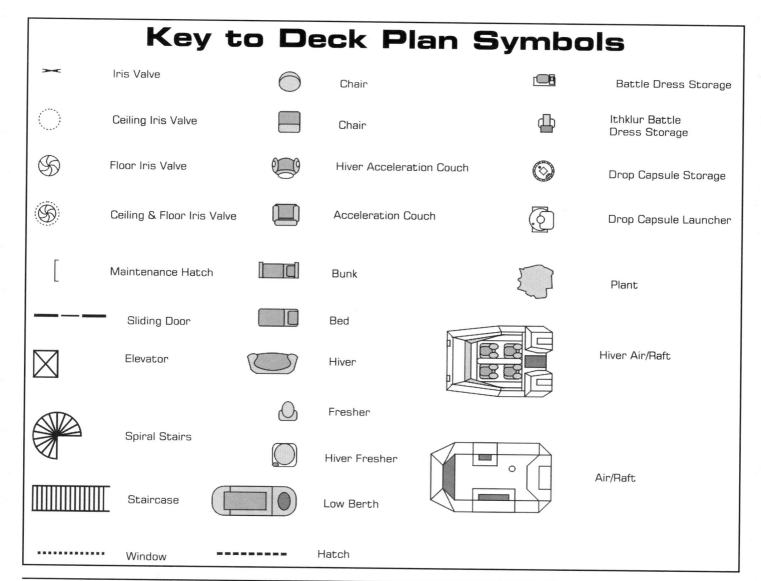

Key to Deck Plan Symbols

⤞	Iris Valve	Chair		Battle Dress Storage
	Ceiling Iris Valve	Chair		Ithklur Battle Dress Storage
	Floor Iris Valve	Hiver Acceleration Couch		Drop Capsule Storage
	Ceiling & Floor Iris Valve	Acceleration Couch		Drop Capsule Launcher
	Maintenance Hatch	Bunk		Plant
	Sliding Door	Bed		
	Elevator	Hiver		Hiver Air/Raft
	Spiral Stairs	Fresher		
		Hiver Fresher		Air/Raft
	Staircase	Low Berth		

Window   Hatch

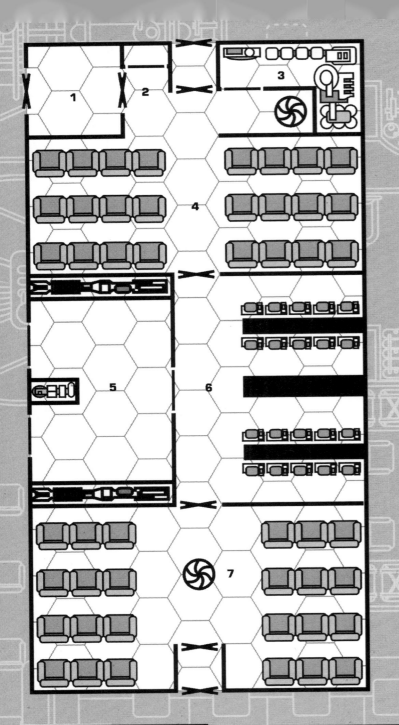

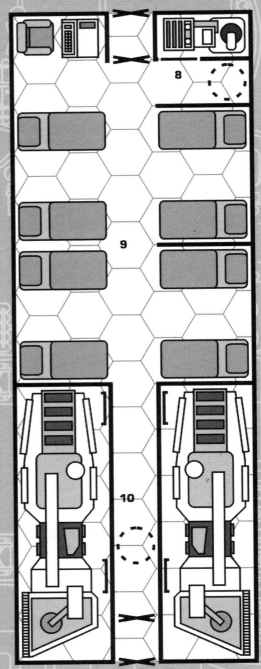

One hex equals one yard.

Symbol key on p. 65

1   2   3

LEGEND

1. Airlock
2. Suit Locker
3. Engineering
4. Team 1 Seating
5. Assault Entry Locks
6. Battledress Morgue
7. Team 2 Seating
8. Life Support
9. Sickbay
10. Drive Access

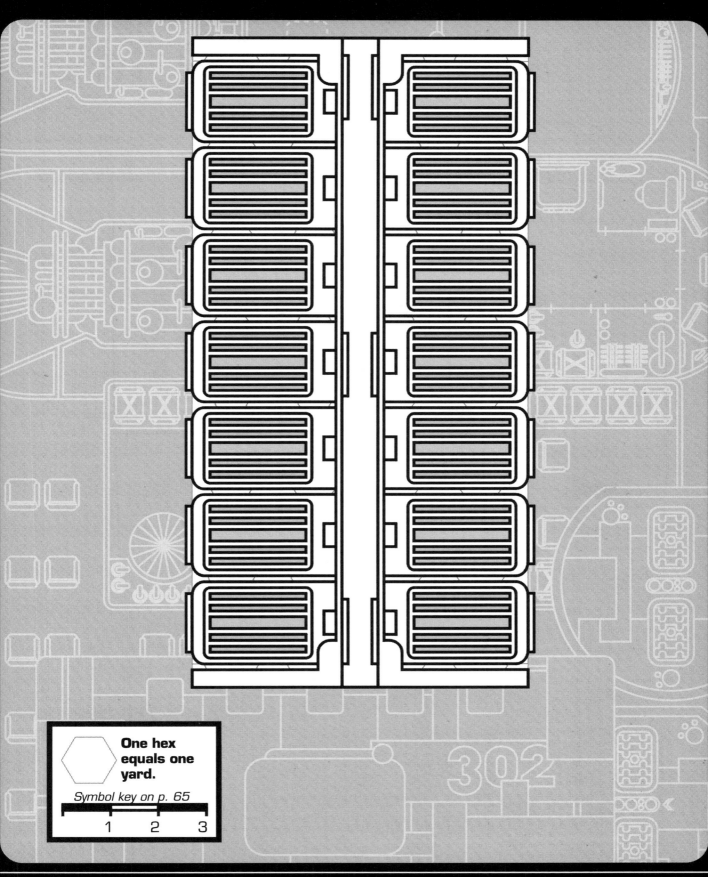

One hex equals one yard.

Symbol key on p. 65

1   2   3

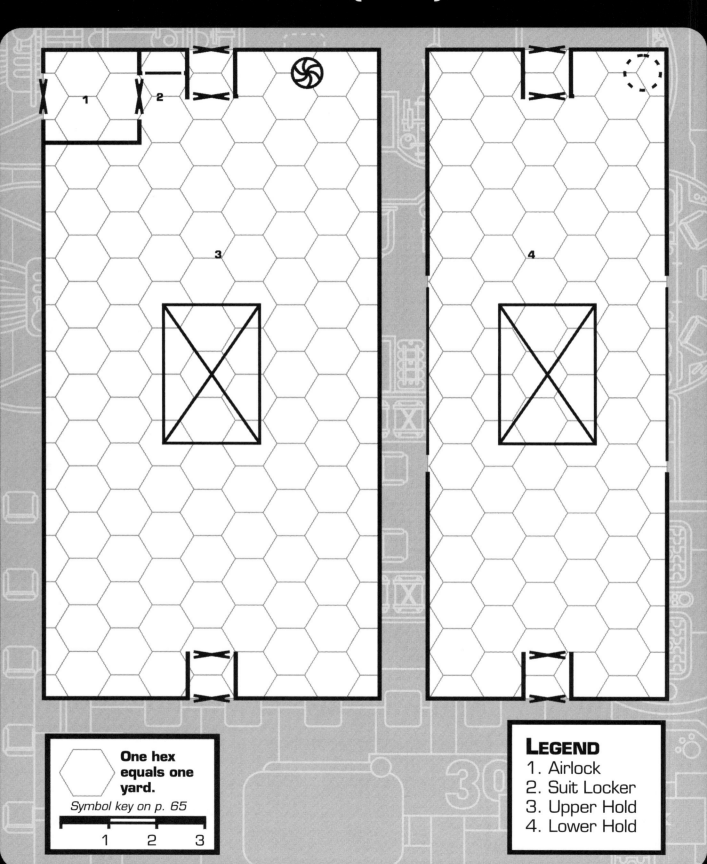

One hex equals one yard.

Symbol key on p. 65

1 2 3

LEGEND
1. Airlock
2. Suit Locker
3. Upper Hold
4. Lower Hold

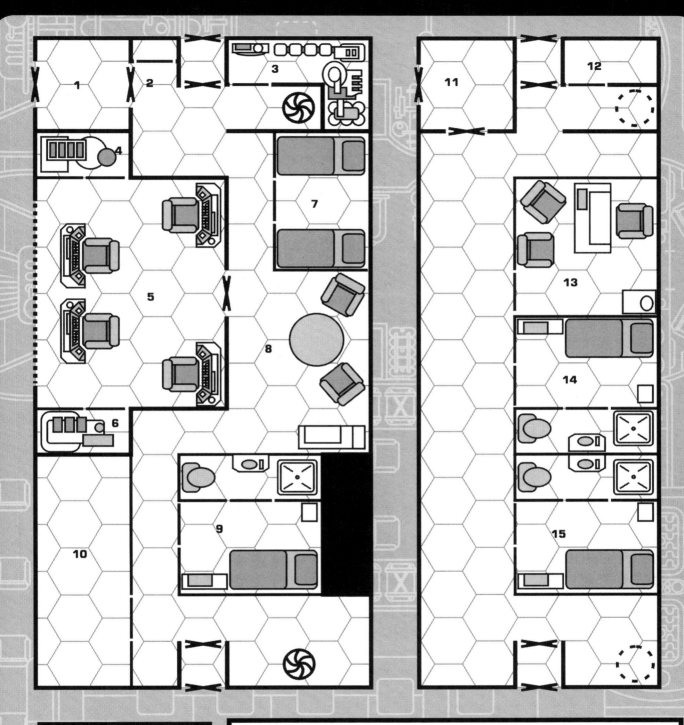

One hex equals one yard.

Symbol key on p. 65

1   2   3

LEGEND

1. Airlock
2. Suit Locker
3. Engineering
4. Communications
5. Flight-Control Room
6. Computer
7. Sickbay
8. Break Area
9. Stateroom
10. Cargo Bay
11. Airlock
12. Storage Closet
13. Office
14-15. Staterooms

COMMUTER (TL10)

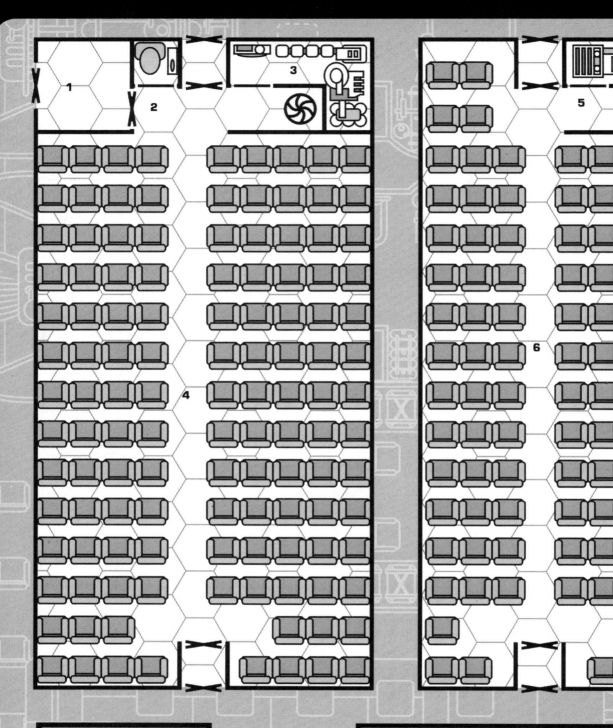

One hex equals one yard.

Symbol key on p. 65

1   2   3

LEGEND
1. Airlock
2. Fresher
3. Engineering
4. Seating
5. Life Support
6. Seating

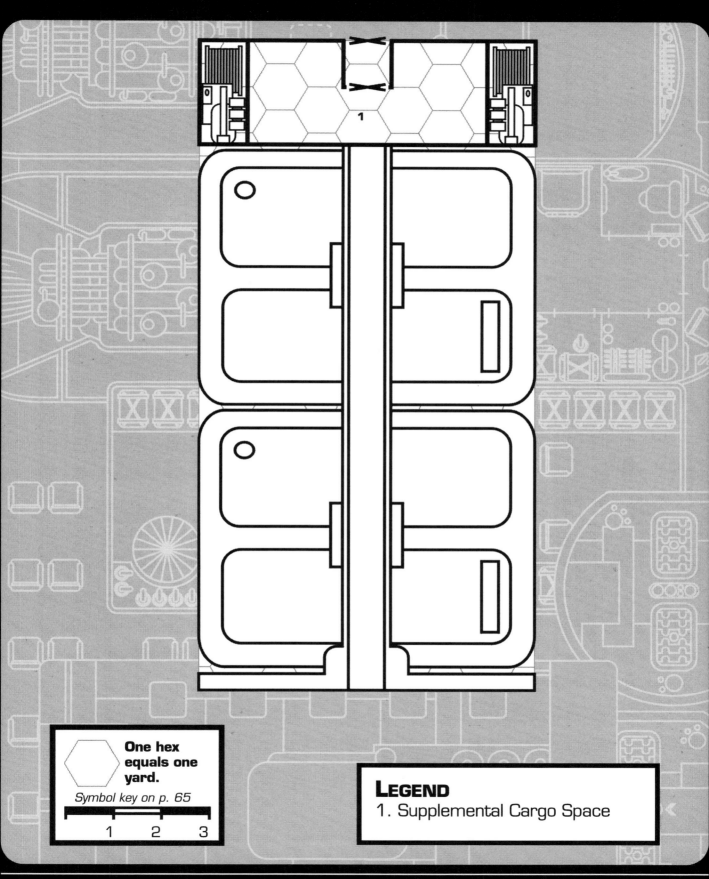

One hex equals one yard.

Symbol key on p. 65

1 2 3

LEGEND

1. Supplemental Cargo Space

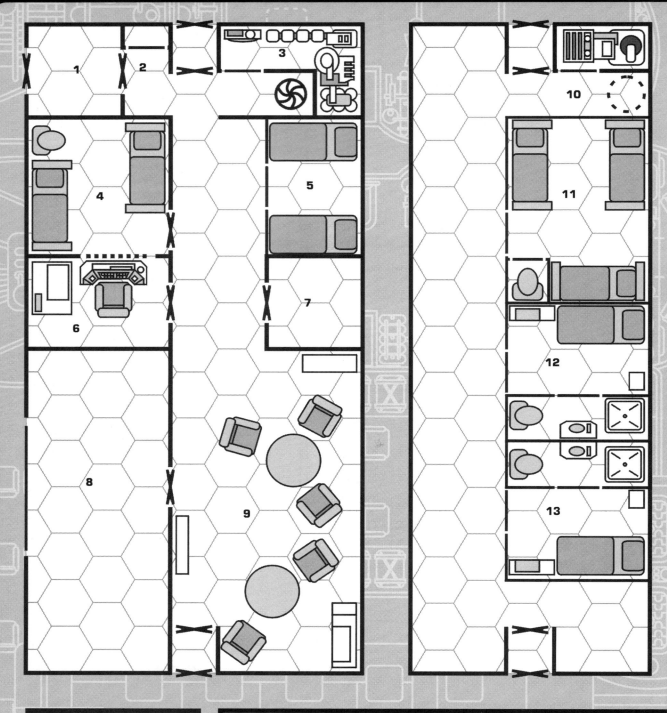

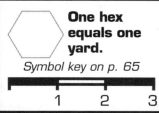

One hex equals one yard.

Symbol key on p. 65

1   2   3

LEGEND

1. Airlock
2. Suit Locker
3. Engineering
4. Brig
5. Sickbay
6. Security Station
7. Armoury/Secure Storage
8. Cargo Hold
9. Break Room
10. Life Support
11. Bunkroom
12-13. Stateroom

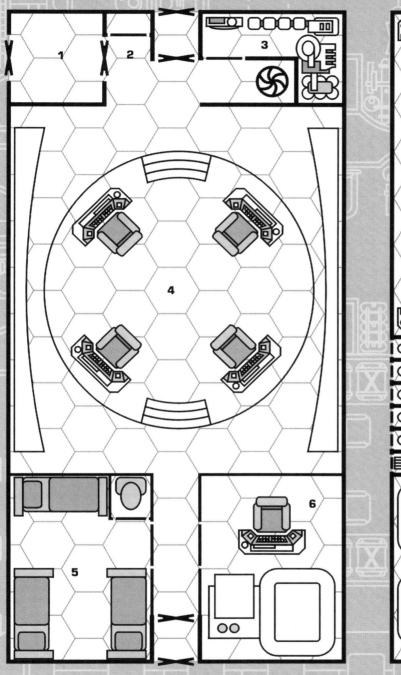

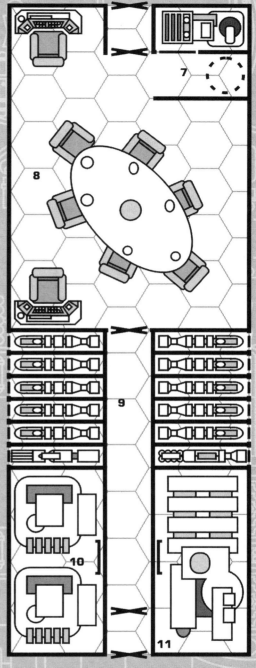

One hex equals one yard.

Symbol key on p. 65

1   2   3

LEGEND

1. Airlock
2. Suit Locker
3. Engineering
4. EW Center
5. Bunkroom
6. Computer Room
7. Life Support
8. Information Center
9. Probe/Missile/ Sand Access
10. Area Jammers
11. Communications

EXPANDABLE BASE (TL12)

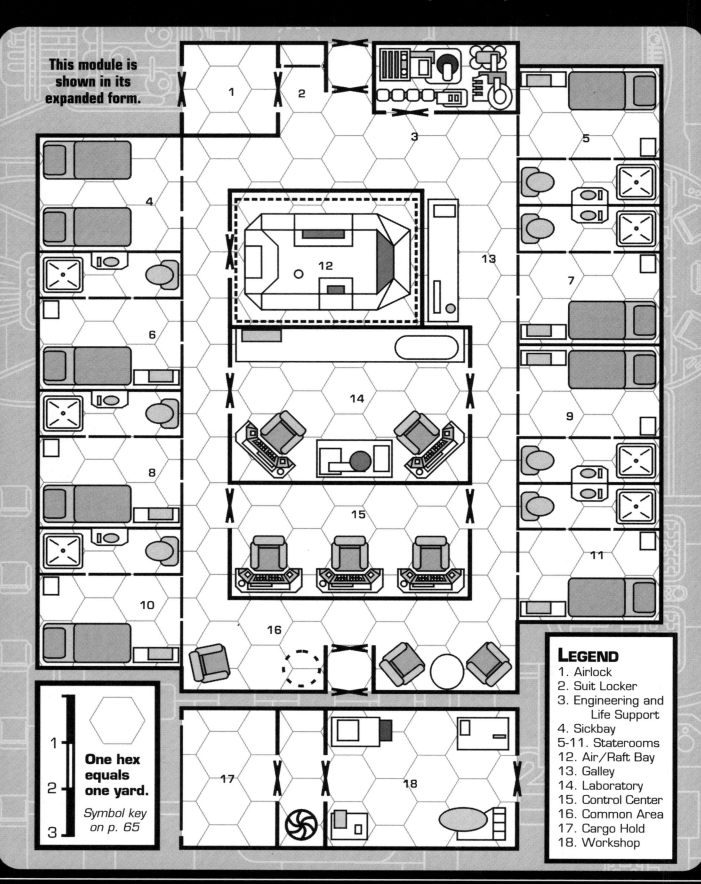

This module is shown in its expanded form.

1 · 2 · 3 · 4 · 5 · 6 · 7 · 8 · 9 · 10 · 11 · 12 · 13 · 14 · 15 · 16 · 17 · 18

1
—
2
—
3

One hex equals one yard.

Symbol key on p. 65

LEGEND
1. Airlock
2. Suit Locker
3. Engineering and Life Support
4. Sickbay
5-11. Staterooms
12. Air/Raft Bay
13. Galley
14. Laboratory
15. Control Center
16. Common Area
17. Cargo Hold
18. Workshop

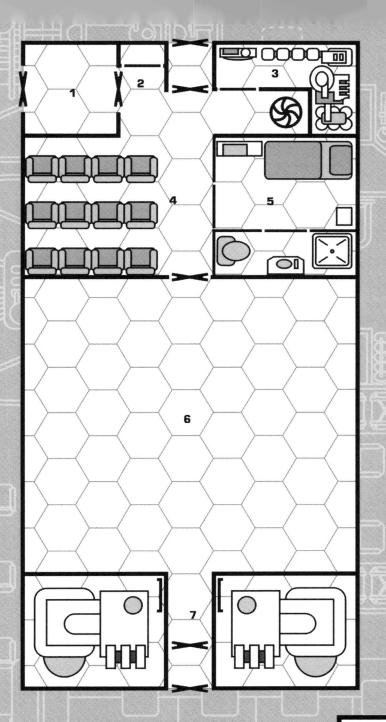

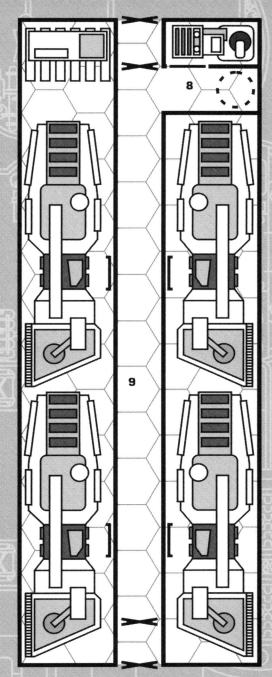

One hex equals one yard.

Symbol key on p. 65

| 1 | 2 | 3 |

LEGEND

1. Airlock
2. Suit locker
3. Engineering
4. Seating
5. Stateroom
6. Cargo
7. Power Plants
8. Life Support
9. Drive Access

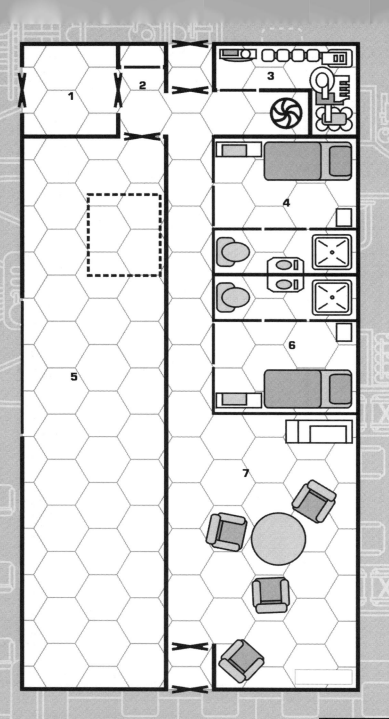

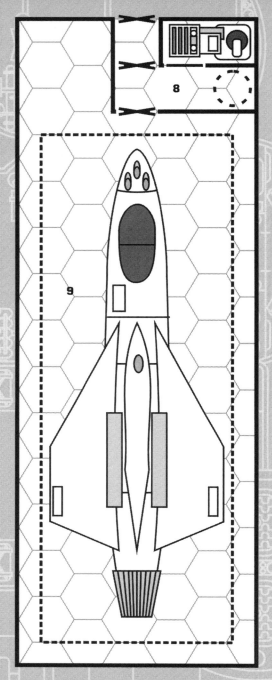

One hex equals one yard.

Symbol key on p. 65

1 2 3

LEGEND

1. Airlock
2. Suit Locker
3. Engineering
4. Stateroom
5. Cargo Hold
6. Stateroom
7. Common Area
8. Life Support
9. Fighter Bay

FIREFIGHTING (TL10)

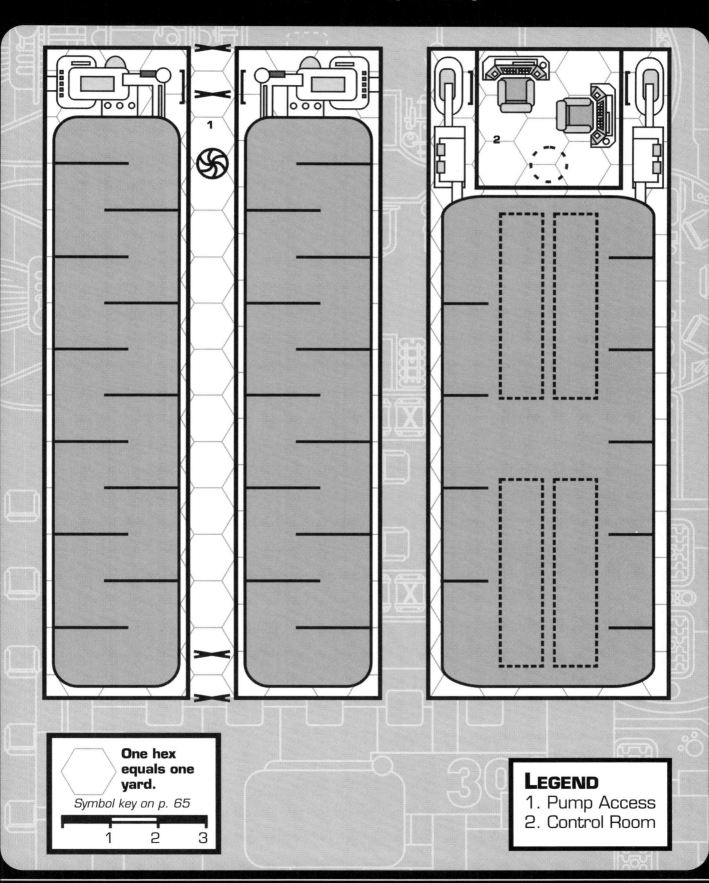

One hex equals one yard.

Symbol key on p. 65

1   2   3

LEGEND
1. Pump Access
2. Control Room

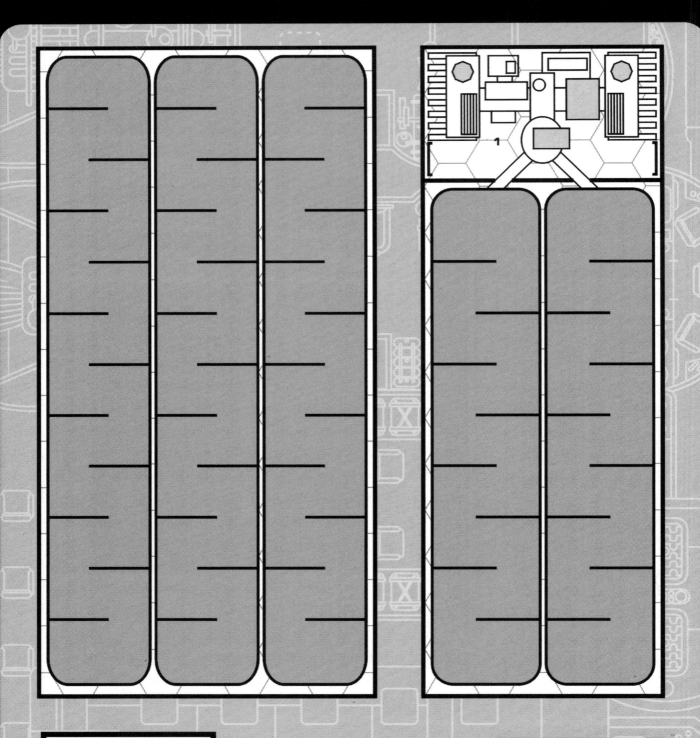

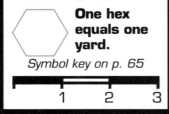

One hex equals one yard.

Symbol key on p. 65

1 2 3

LEGEND
1. Skimming and Pumping Equipment

GARAGE (ATV) (TL10)

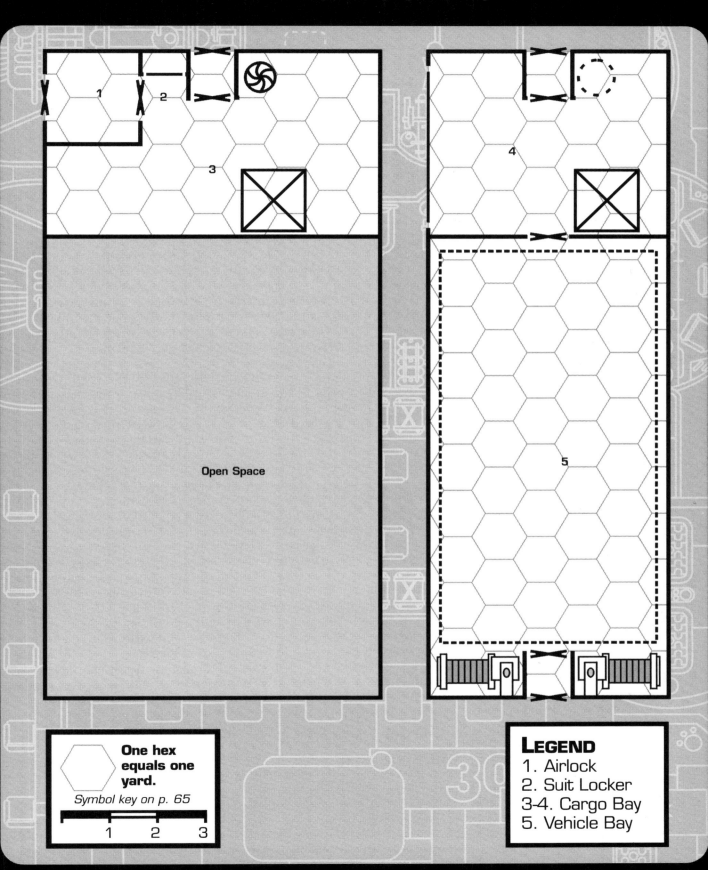

Open Space

One hex equals one yard.
Symbol key on p. 65

1 2 3

LEGEND
1. Airlock
2. Suit Locker
3-4. Cargo Bay
5. Vehicle Bay

MODULES   79

High-Capacity Berthing (TL10)

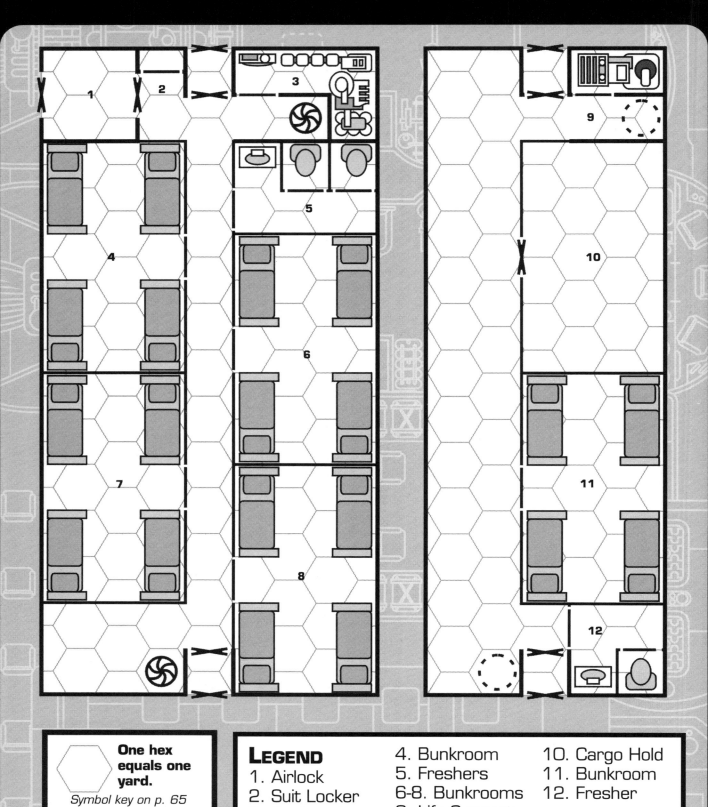

One hex equals one yard.

Symbol key on p. 65

1   2   3

LEGEND
1. Airlock
2. Suit Locker
3. Engineering
4. Bunkroom
5. Freshers
6-8. Bunkrooms
9. Life Support
10. Cargo Hold
11. Bunkroom
12. Fresher

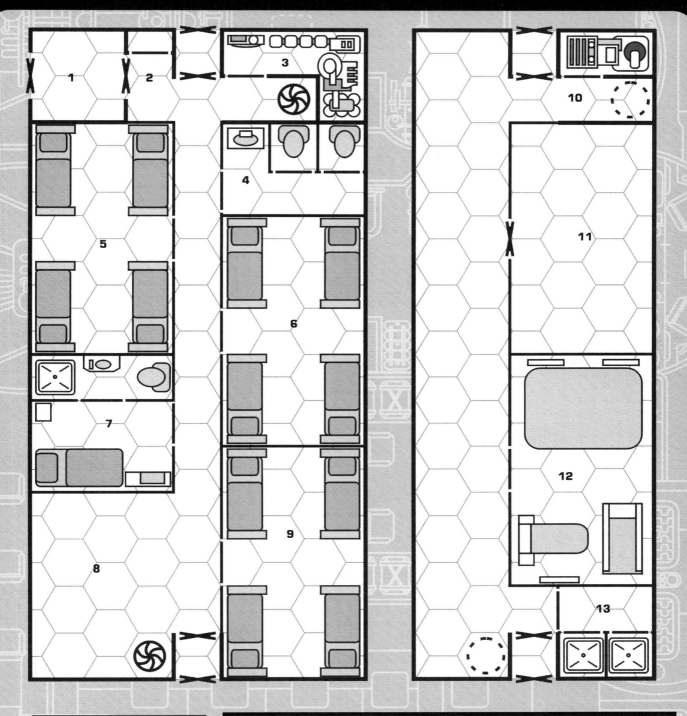

One hex equals one yard.

Symbol key on p. 65

1   2   3

LEGEND

1. Airlock
2. Suit Locker
3. Engineering
4. Freshers
5-6. Bunkrooms
7. Stateroom
8. Common Area
9. Bunkroom
10. Life Support
11. Cargo Hold
12. Gymnasium
13. Showers

LABORATORY (TL10)

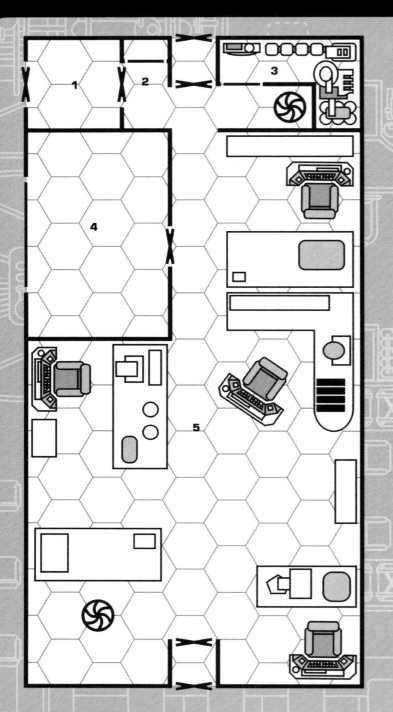
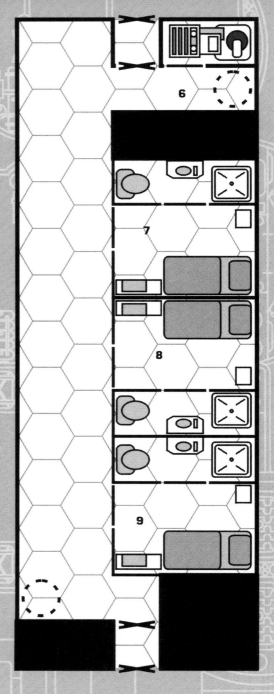

One hex equals one yard.

Symbol key on p. 65

1   2   3

LEGEND
1. Airlock
2. Suit Locker
3. Engineering
4. Cargo Bay
5. Lab
6. Life Support
7-9. Staterooms

Logistics (TL10)

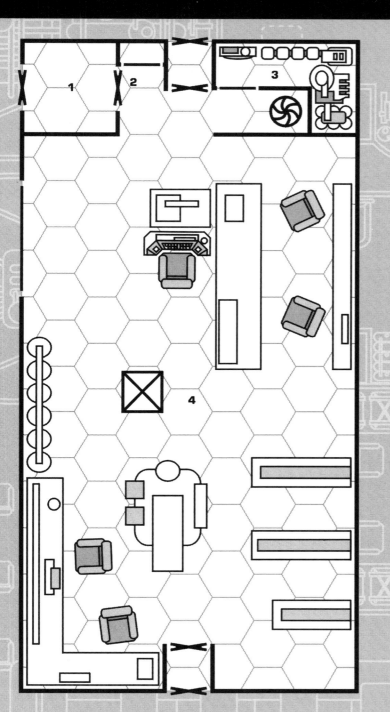

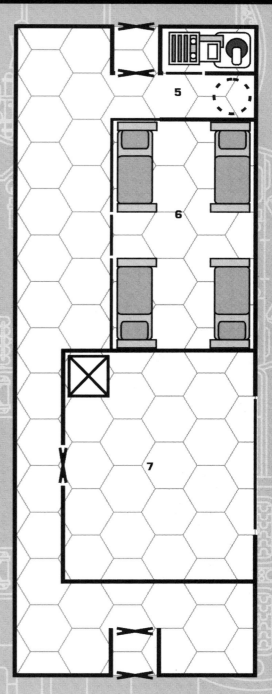

One hex equals one yard.

Symbol key on p. 65

1   2   3

LEGEND

1. Airlock
2. Suit Locker
3. Engineering
4. Workshop
5. Life Support
6. Bunkroom
7. Cargo Bay

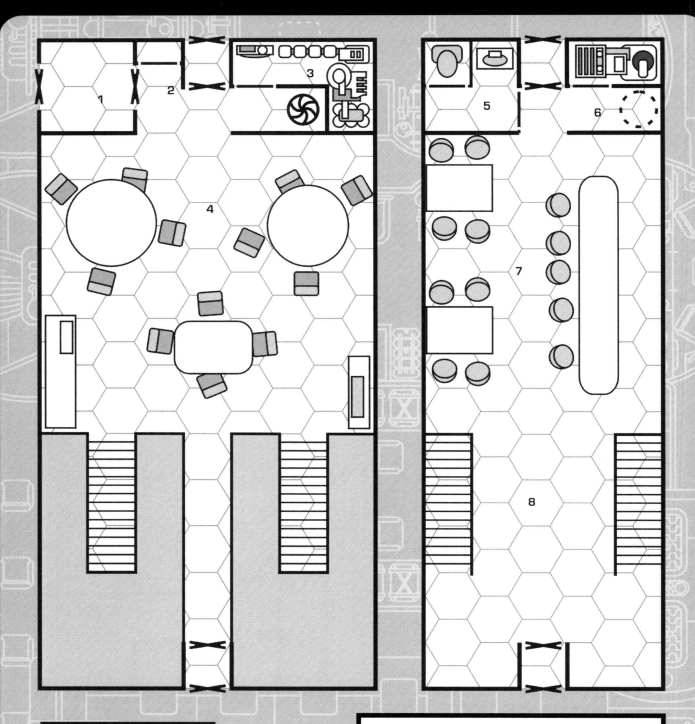

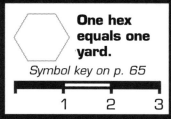

One hex equals one yard.

Symbol key on p. 65

1   2   3

LEGEND

1. Airlock
2. Suit Locker
3. Engineering
4. Dining Area
5. Fresher
6. Life Support
7. Bar
8. Dance Floor/ Open Area

Low Berth (TL10)

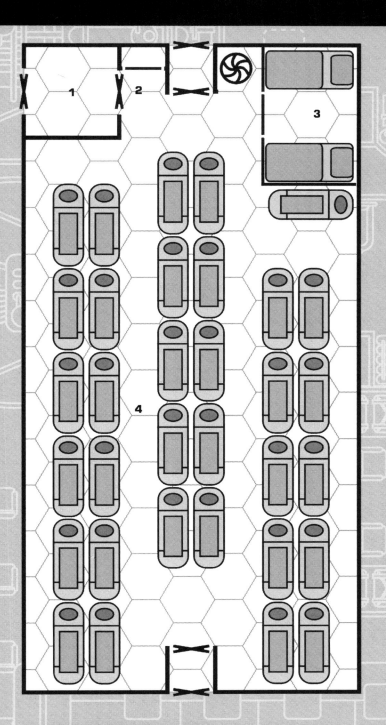
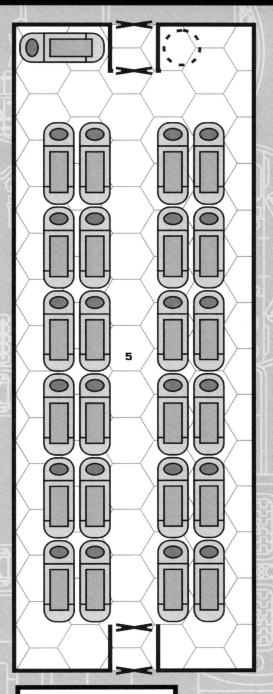

Symbol key on p. 65

One hex
equals one
yard.

1 2 3

Legend

1. Airlock
2. Suit Locker
3. Sickbay
4. Berths
5. Berths

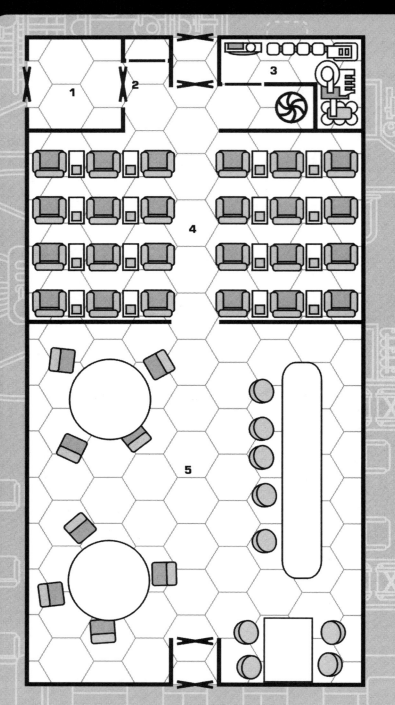

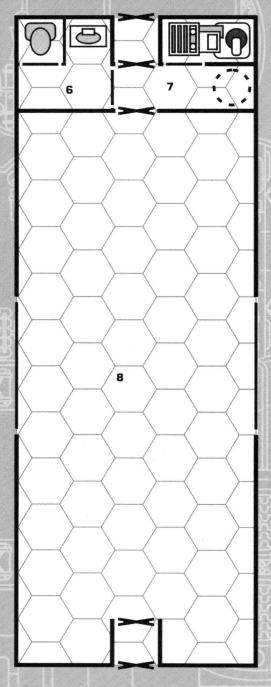

One hex equals one yard.

Symbol key on p. 65

1 2 3

LEGEND

1. Airlock
2. Suit Locker
3. Engineering
4. Seating

5, Dining/
  Bar Area
6. Fresher
7. Life Support
8. Cargo Bay

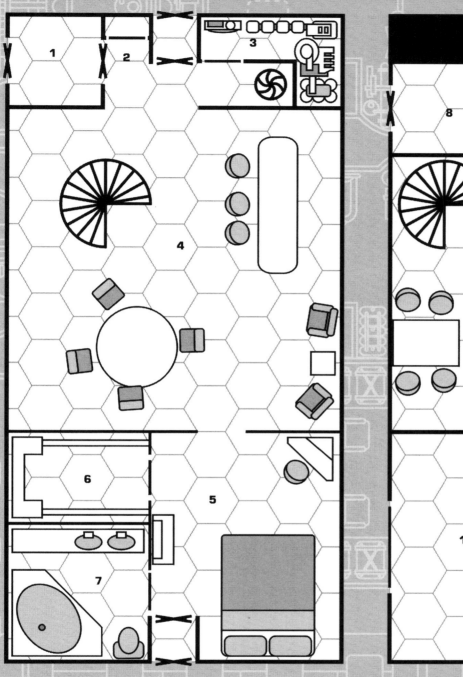

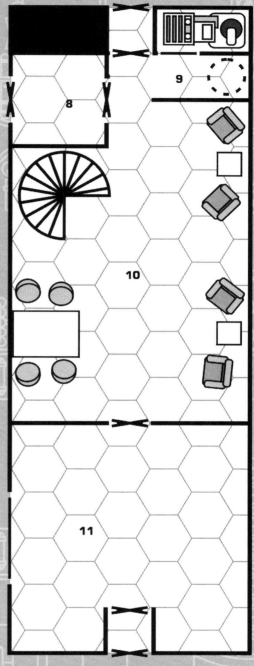

One hex equals one yard.

Symbol key on p. 65

1   2   3

LEGEND

1. Airlock
2. Suit Locker
3. Engineering
4. Dining/ Bar Area
5. Master Bedroom
6. Closet
7. Fresher
8. Airlock
9. Life Support
10. Lounge
11. Cargo Bay

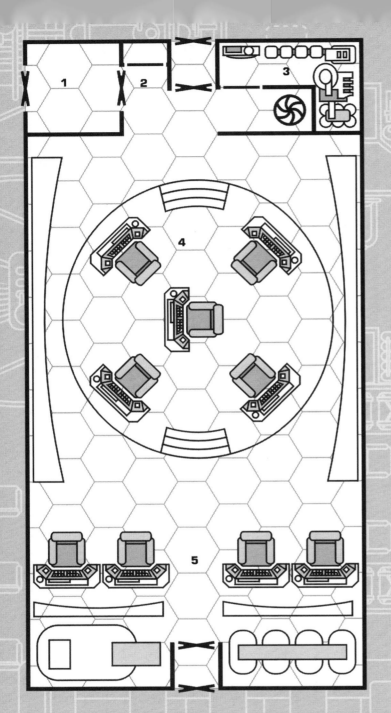

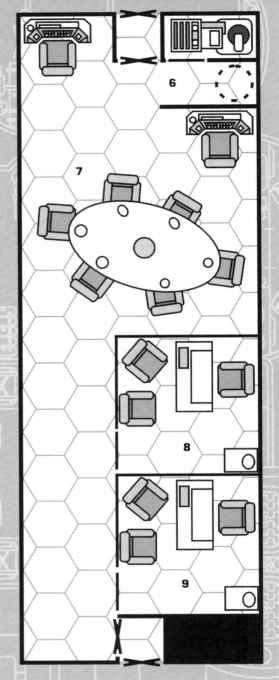

One hex equals one yard.

Symbol key on p. 65

| 1 | 2 | 3 |

LEGEND

1. Airlock
2. Suit Locker
3. Engineering

4. Command Center
5. Flight Control

6. Life Support
7. Information Center
8-9. Offices

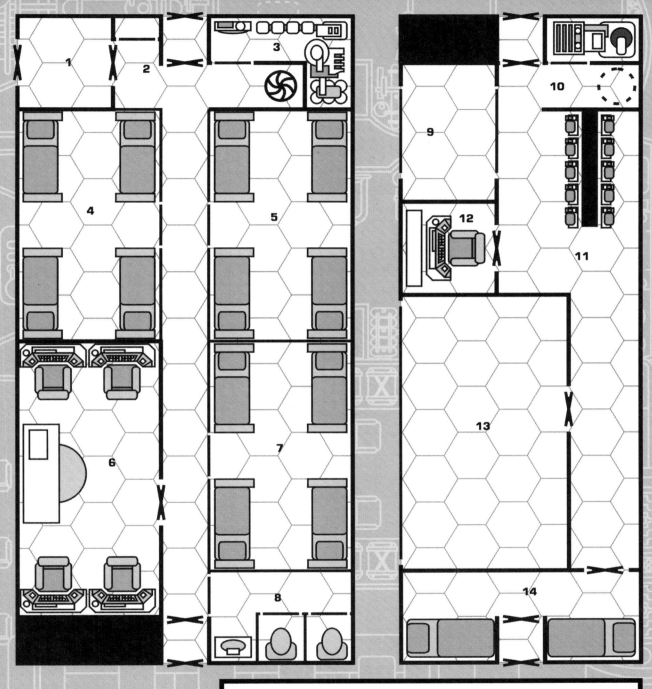

One hex equals one yard.

Symbol key on p. 65

1   2   3

LEGEND

1. Airlock
2. Suit Locker
3. Engineering
4-5. Bunkrooms
6. Command Center
7. Bunkroom
8. Freshers
9. Lower Assault Lock
10. Life Support
11. Battledress Morgue
12. Turret Control
13. Vehicle Bay
14. Sickbay

MEDEVAC (TL10)

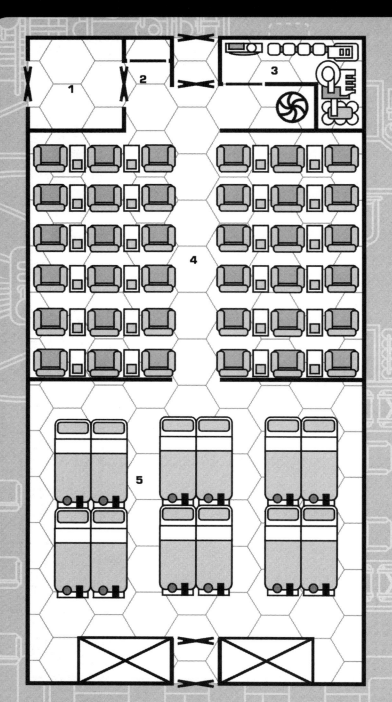

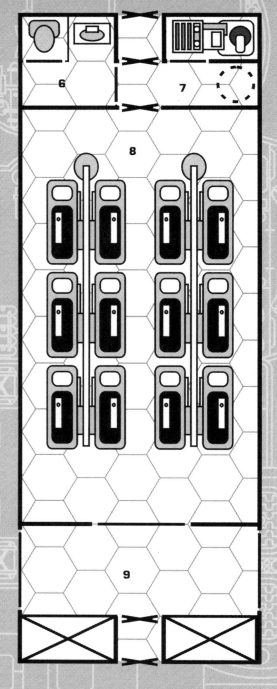

One hex equals one yard.

Symbol key on p. 65

1   2   3

LEGEND

1. Airlock
2. Suit Locker
3. Engineering
4. Seating
5. Stretcher Racks
6. Fresher
7. Life Support
8. Automed Racks
9. Primary Airlock

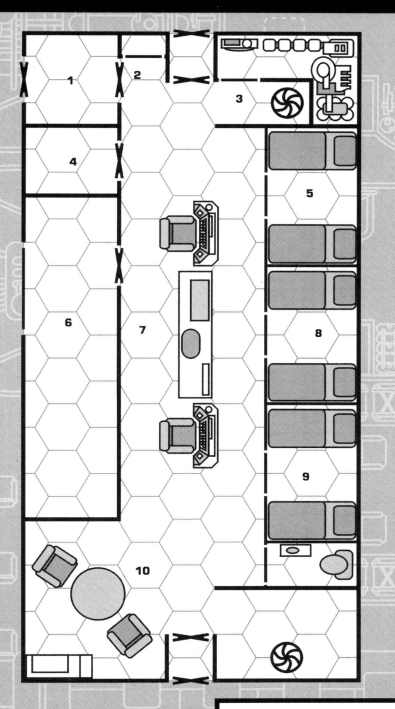
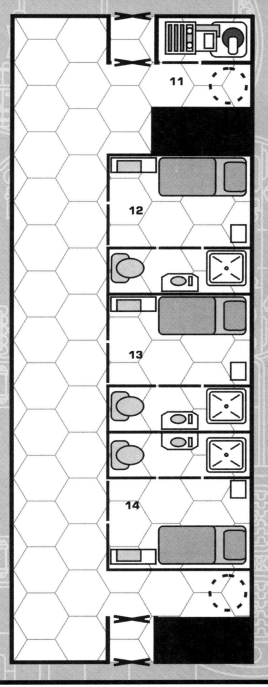

One hex equals one yard.

Symbol key on p. 65

1 2 3

LEGEND
1. Airlock
2. Suit Locker
3. Engineering
4. Drug Closet
5. Patient Room
6. Cargo Bay
7. Nurse's Station
8-9. Patient Rooms
10. Break Area
11. Life Support
12-14. Staterooms

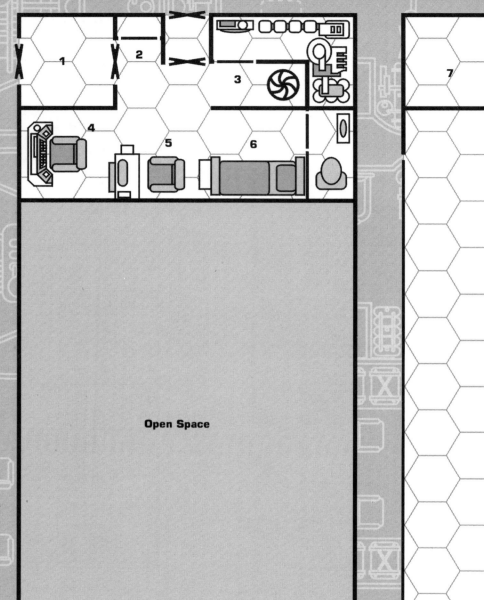

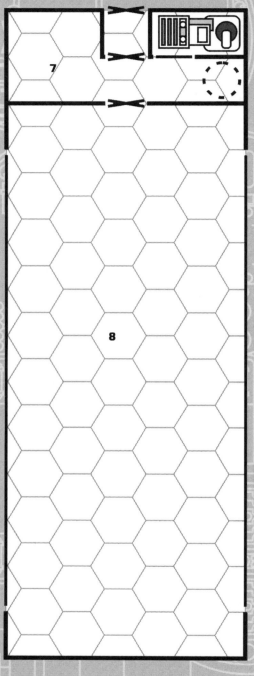

Open Space

8

One hex equals one yard.

Symbol key on p. 65

1   2   3

LEGEND

1. Airlock
2. Suit Locker
3. Engineering
4. Laser Controls
5. Mineral Lab
6. Bunks
7. Cargo Bay
8. Ore Bay

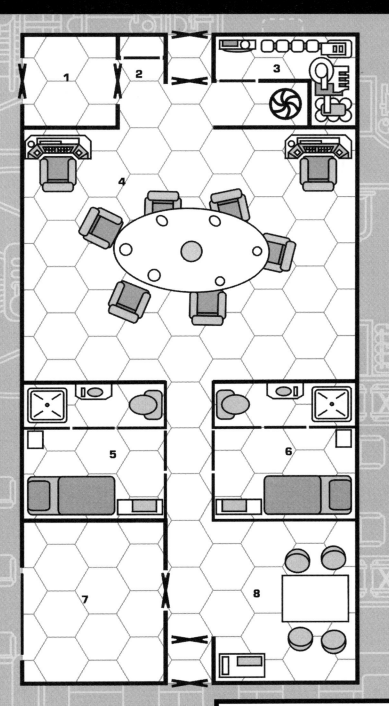

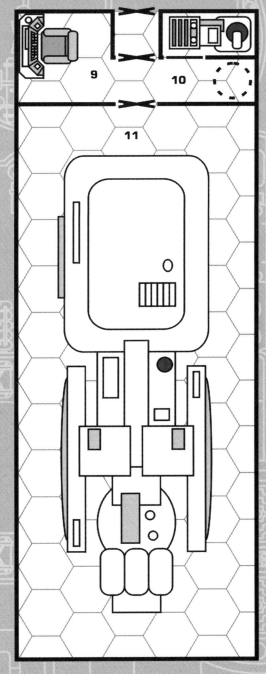

One hex equals one yard.

Symbol key on p. 65

1   2   3

Legend
1. Airlock
2. Suit Locker
3. Engineering
4. Information Center
5-6. Staterooms
7. Cargo Bay
8. Break Room
9. Damper Controls
10. Life Support
11. Damper Machinery

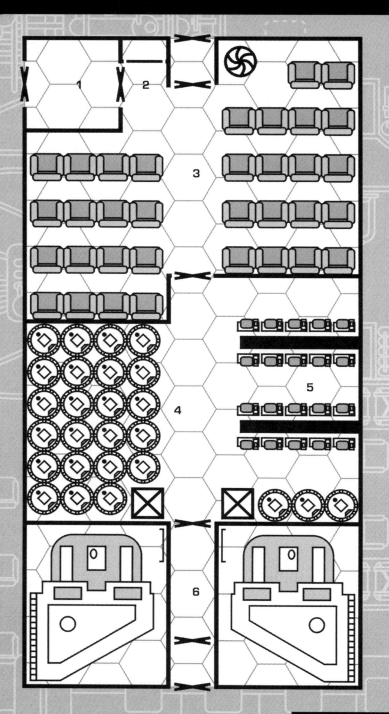

One hex equals one yard.

Symbol key on p. 65

1 2 3

LEGEND

1. Airlock
2. Suit Locker
3. Troop Seating
4. Capsule Storage
5. Battledress Morgue
6. Drive Access
7. Launcher Assemblies

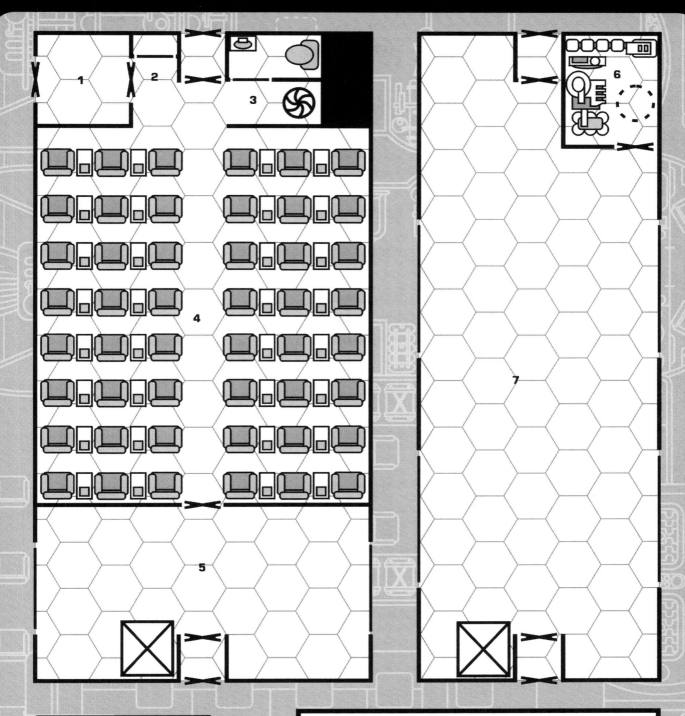

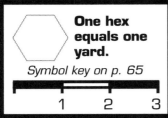

One hex equals one yard.

Symbol key on p. 65

1   2   3

LEGEND

1. Airlock
2. Suit Locker
3. Fresher
4. Seating
5. Upper Cargo Bay
6. Engineering and Life Support
7. Lower Cargo Bay

PLANETARY INFRASTRUCTURE (TL10)

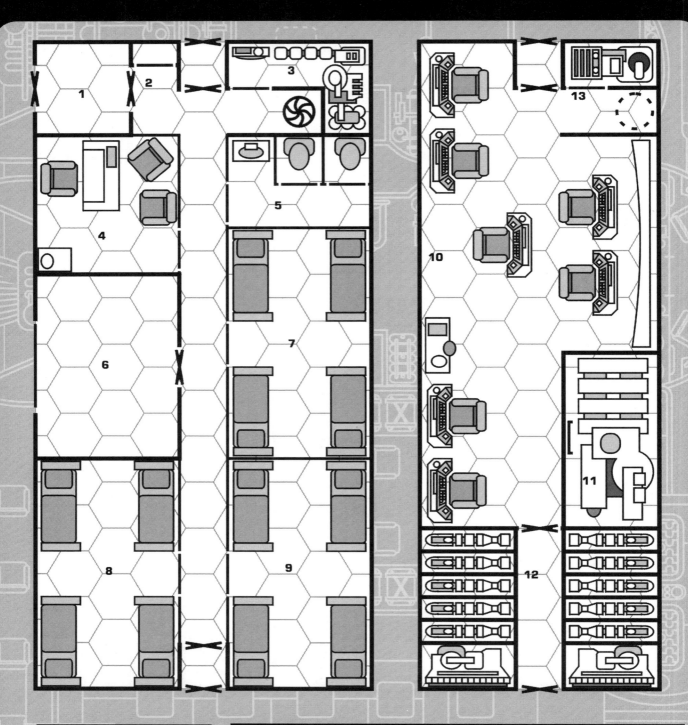

Symbol key on p. 65

One hex equals one yard.

LEGEND
1. Airlock
2. Suit Locker
3. Engineering
4. Office
5. Fresher
6. Cargo Bay
7-9. Bunkrooms
10. Flight-Control Center
11. Communications Array
12. Satellite and Drive Access
13. Life Support

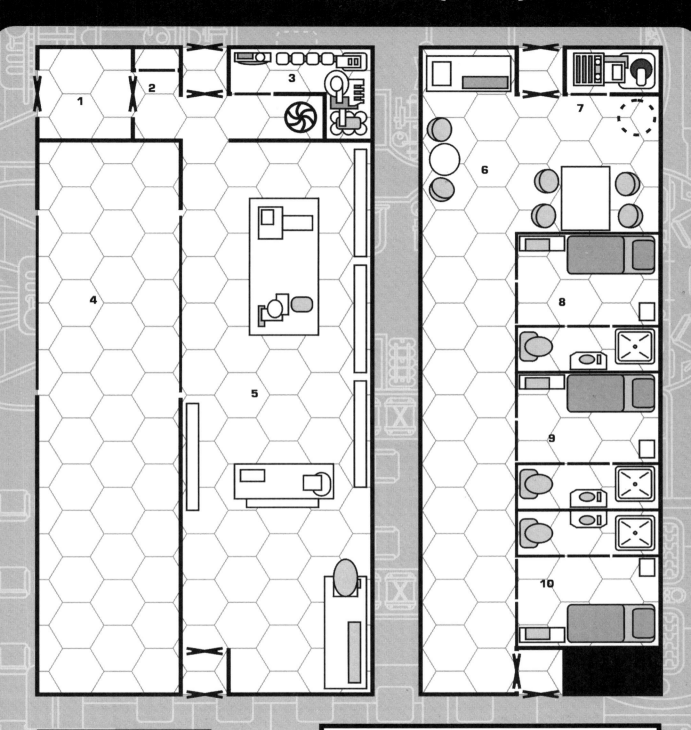

One hex equals one yard.

Symbol key on p. 65

1   2   3

LEGEND

1. Airlock
2. Suit Locker
3. Engineering
4. Cargo Hold
5. Workshop
6. Break Area
7. Life Support
8-10. Staterooms

PRISON TRANSPORT (TL10)

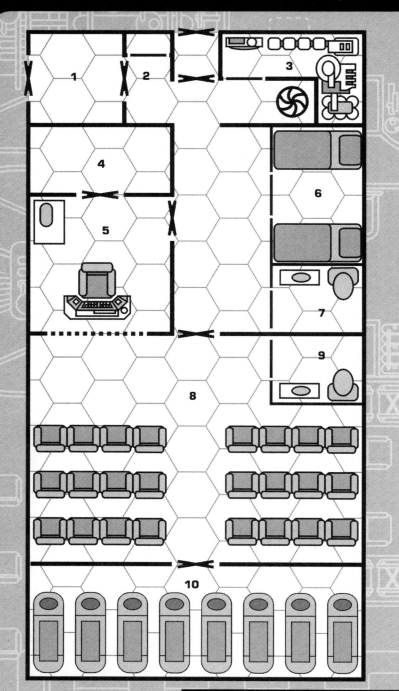

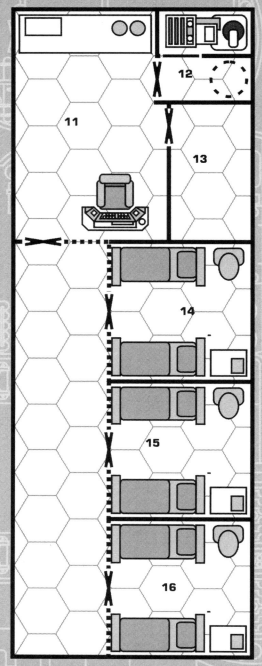

One hex equals one yard.

Symbol key on p. 65

1   2   3

LEGEND

1. Airlock
2. Suit Locker
3. Engineering
4. Security Locker
5. Security Station
6. Sickbay
7. Guard Fresher
8. Minimum Security Seating
9. Prisoner Fresher
10. Maximum-Security Low Berths
11. Security Station
12. Life Support
13. Security Locker
14-16. Medium-Security Brigs

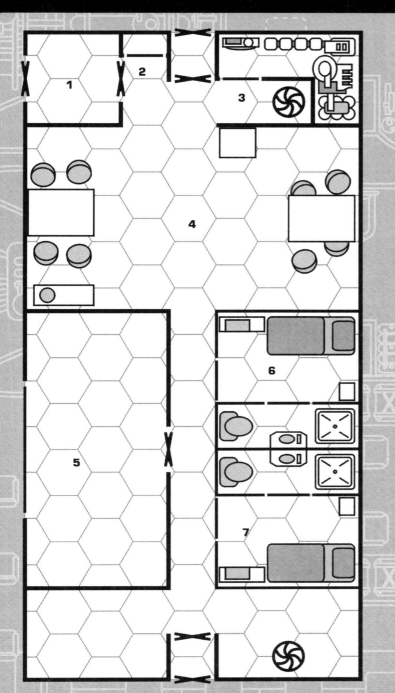

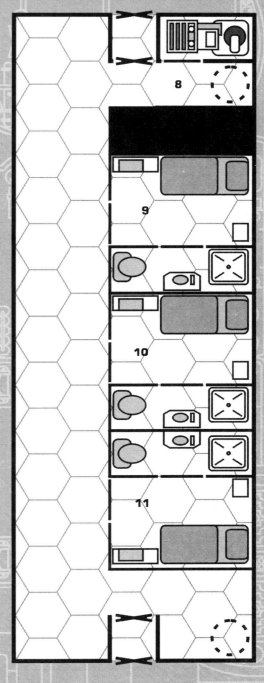

One hex equals one yard.

Symbol key on p. 65

1 2 3

LEGEND

1. Airlock
2. Suit Locker
3. Engineering
4. Common Area
5. Cargo Hold
6-7. Staterooms
8. Life Support
9-11. Staterooms

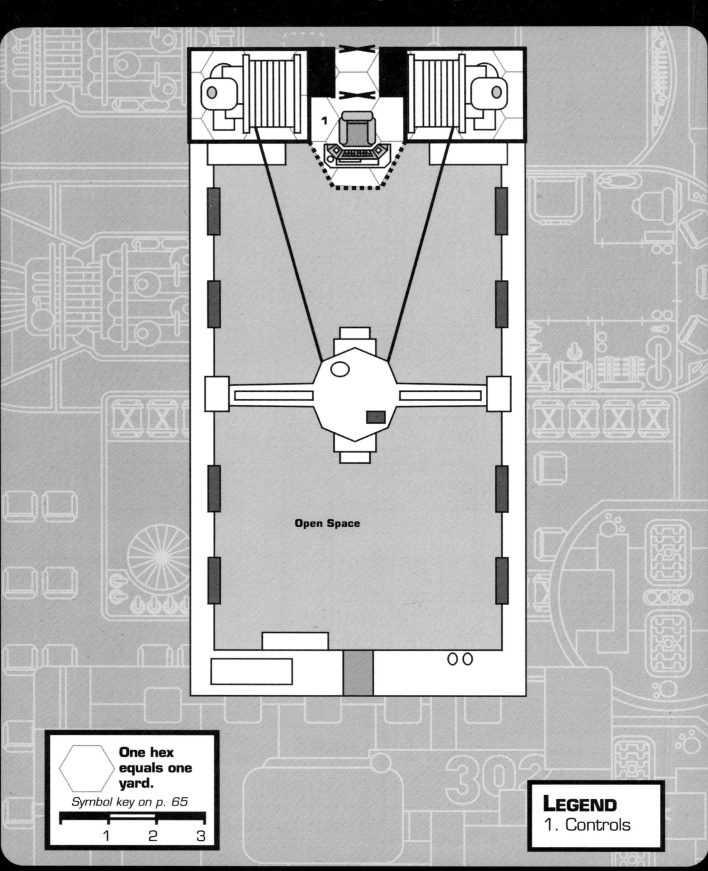

Open Space

One hex equals one yard.

Symbol key on p. 65

1   2   3

LEGEND
1. Controls

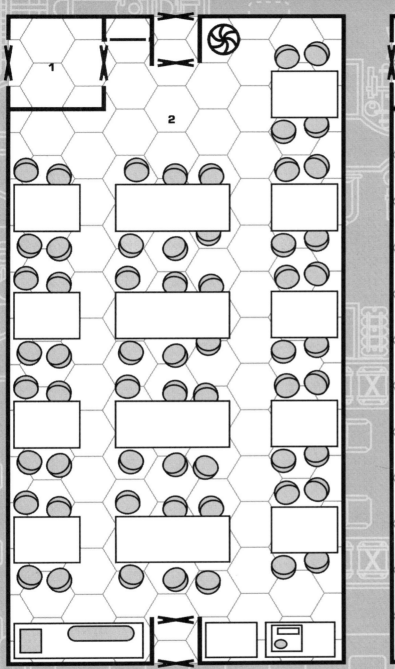

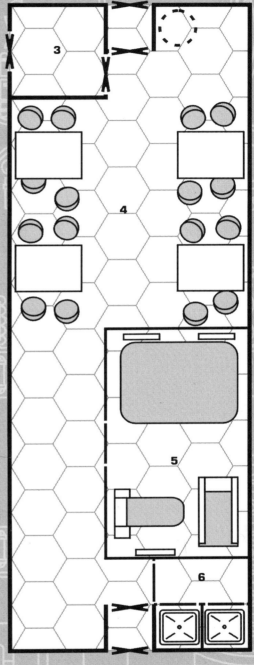

One hex equals one yard.

Symbol key on p. 65

1   2   3

LEGEND
1. Airlock
2. Cafeteria/Dining
3. Airlock
4. Cafeteria/Dining
5. Gymnasium
6. Showers

SAFARI (TL10)

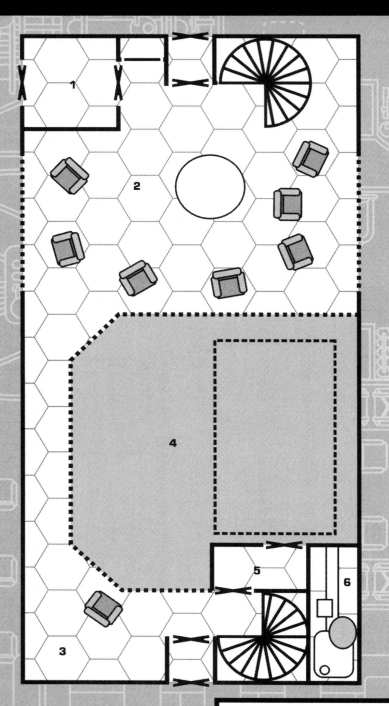

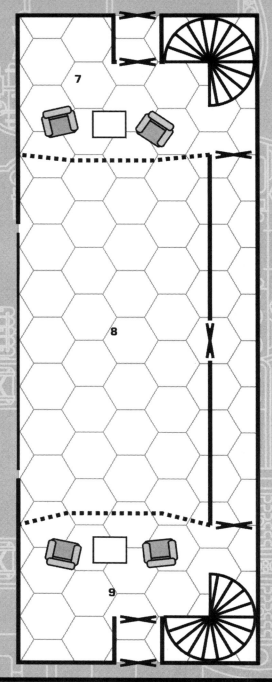

One hex equals one yard.

Symbol key on p. 65

1   2   3

LEGEND

1. Airlock
2. Observation Lounge
3. Aquarium Lounge
4. Aquarium
5. Wetlock
6. Pump Machinery
7. Containment Lounge
8. Animal Containment
9. Containment Lounge

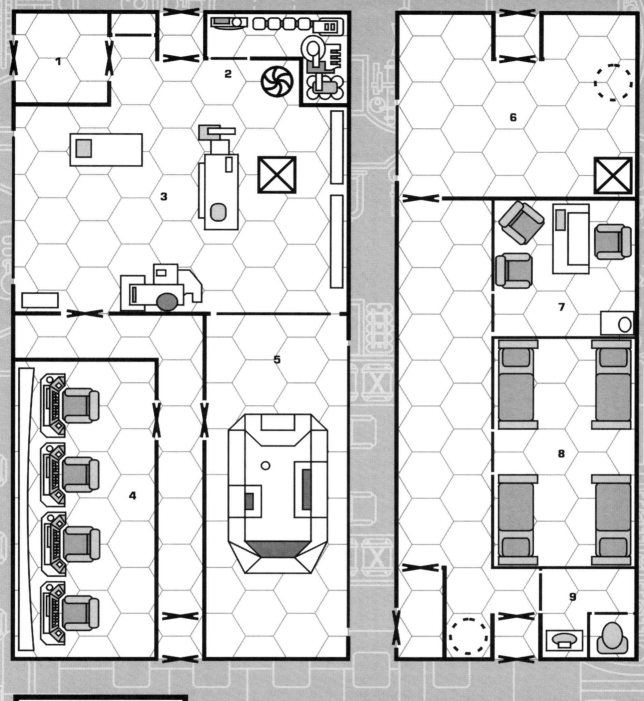

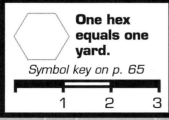

One hex equals one yard.

Symbol key on p. 65

1   2   3

LEGEND
1. Airlock
2. Engineering
3. Workshop
4. Flight-Control Center
5. Air/Raft Bay
6. Cargo Bay
7. Office
8. Bunkroom
9. Fresher

SCOUT SURVEY BASE (TL10)

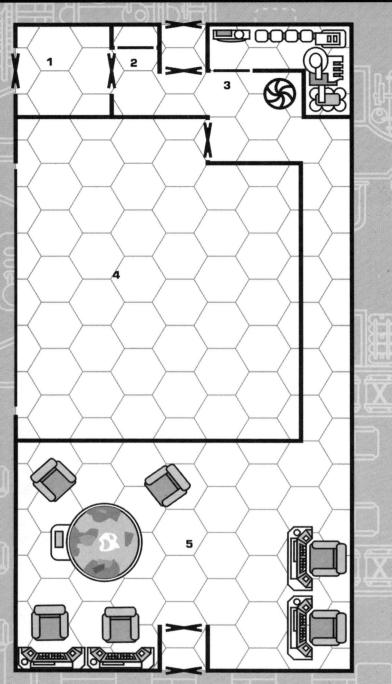

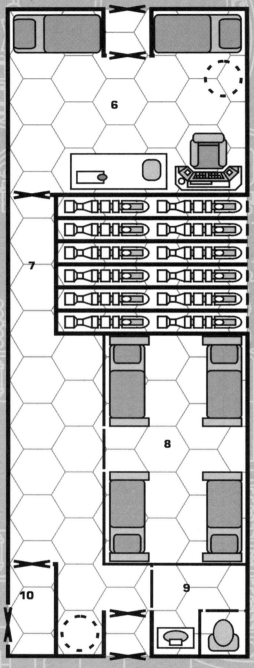

One hex equals one yard.

Symbol key on p. 65

1   2   3

LEGEND

1. Airlock
2. Suit locker
3. Engineering
4. Vehicle Bay
5. Survey Center
6. Laboratory/ Sickbay
7. Probe Access
8. Bunkroom
9. Fresher
10. Airlock

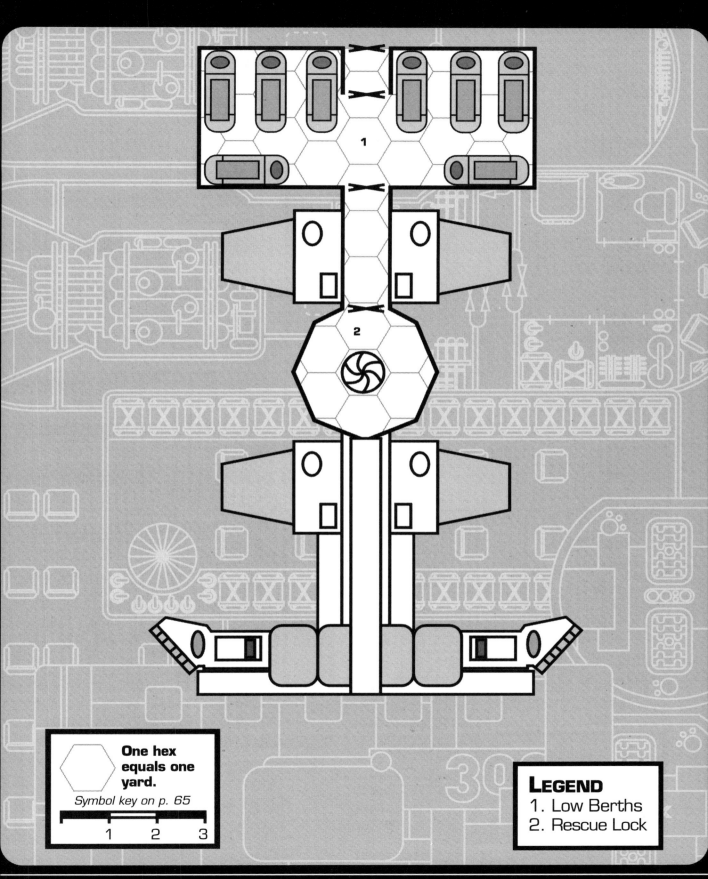

One hex
equals one
yard.

Symbol key on p. 65

1   2   3

LEGEND
1. Low Berths
2. Rescue Lock

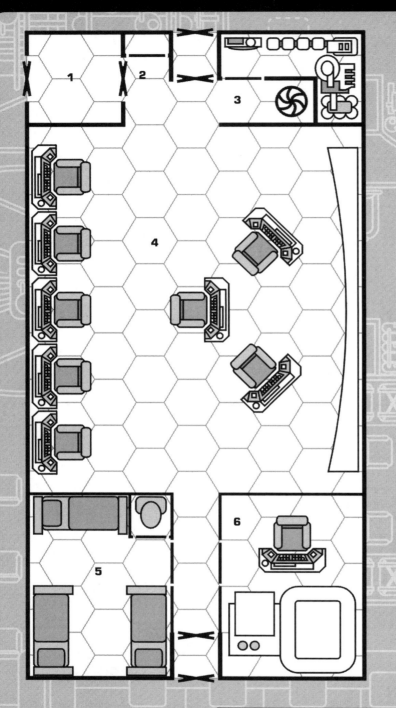

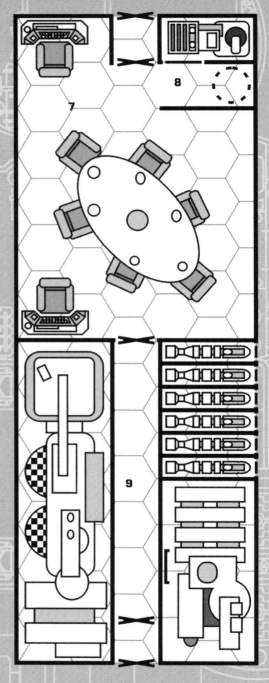

One hex equals one yard.

Symbol key on p. 65

1 2 3

LEGEND
1. Airlock
2. Suit Locker
3. Engineering
4. Control Center
5. Bunkroom
6. Computer Room
7. Information Center
8. Life Support
9. Probe and Sensor Access

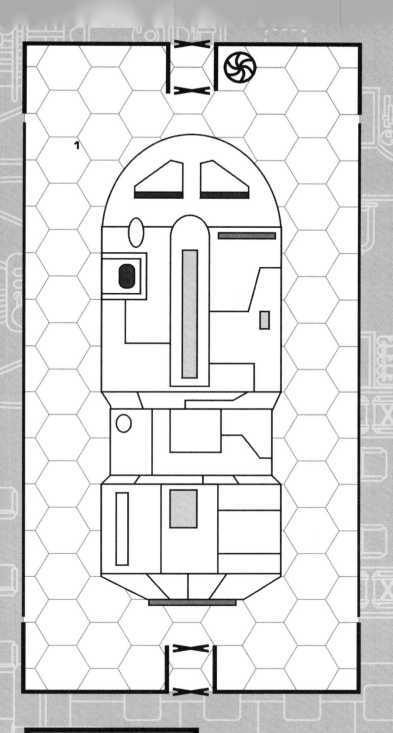

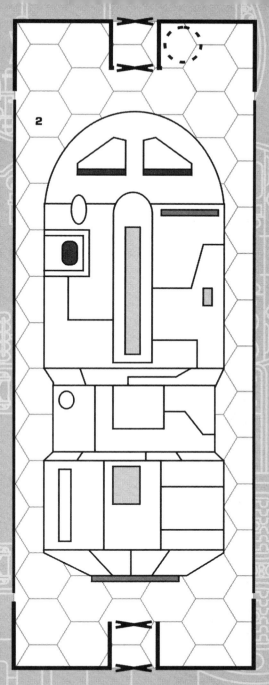

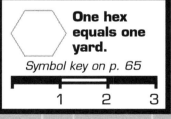

One hex equals one yard.

Symbol key on p. 65

1   2   3

LEGEND

1. Upper Boat Bay
2. Lower Boat Bay

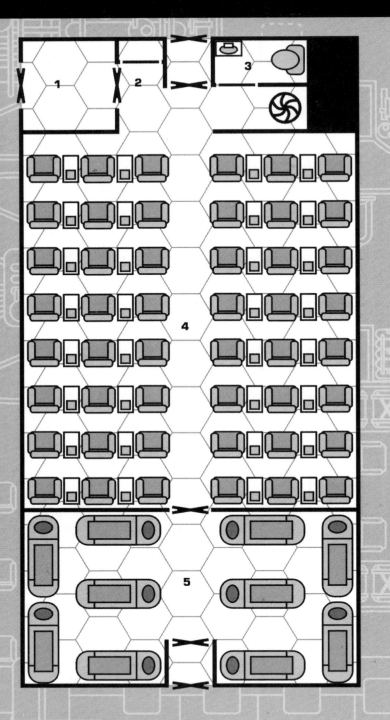

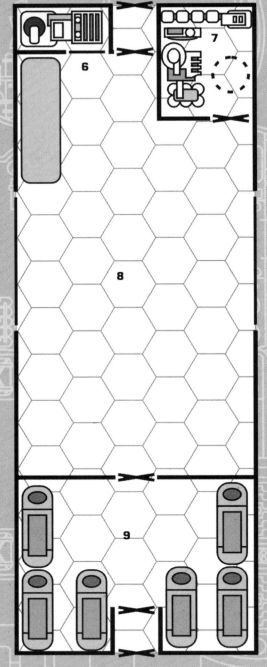

LEGEND

1. Airlock
2. Suit Locker
3. Fresher
4. Seating
5. Low Berths
6. Life Support
7. Engineering
8. Cargo Bay, Collapsible Fuel Tank
9. Low Berths

SURVEY (TL10)

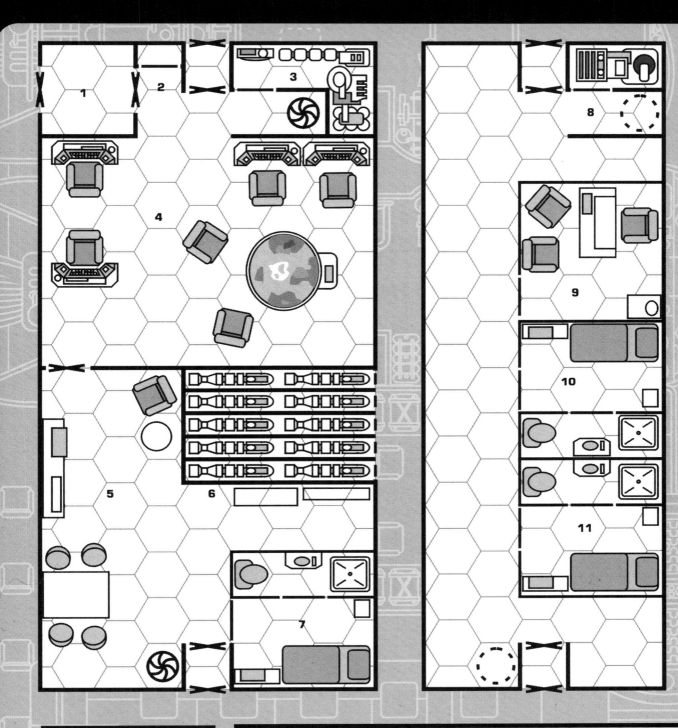

One hex equals one yard.

Symbol key on p. 65

1   2   3

LEGEND

1. Airlock
2. Suit Locker
3. Engineering
4. Survey Center
5. Common Area
6. Probe Access
7. Stateroom
8. Life Support
9. Office
10 -11. Staterooms

THEATER (TL10)

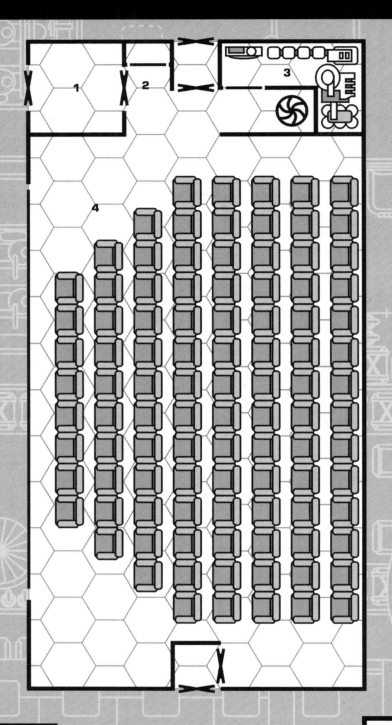

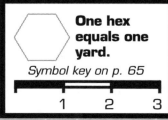

One hex equals one yard.
Symbol key on p. 65

1 2 3

LEGEND
1. Airlock
2. Suit Locker
3. Engineering
4. Seating

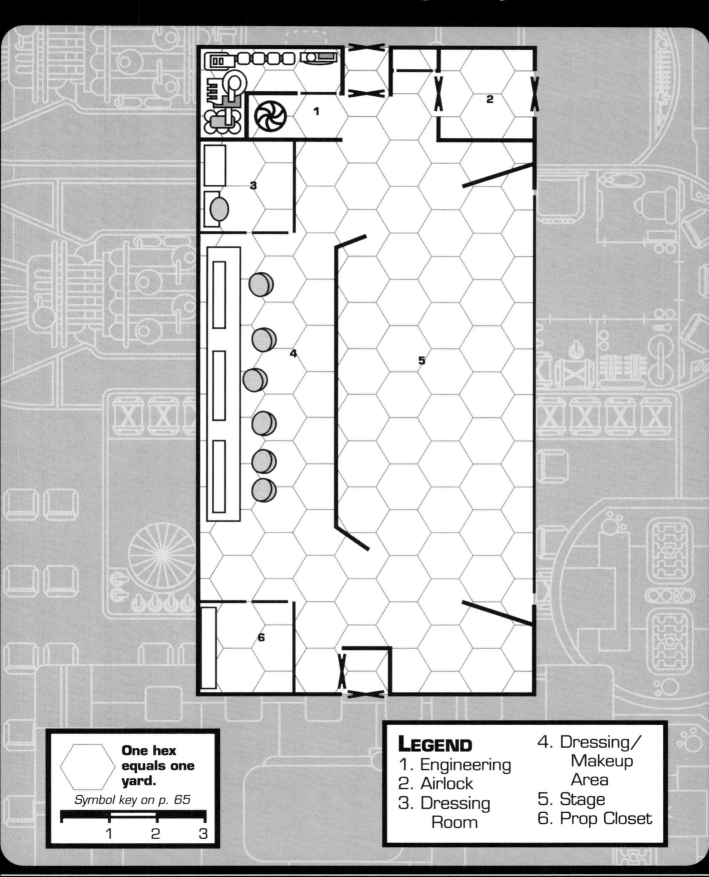

One hex equals one yard.

Symbol key on p. 65

1 2 3

LEGEND

1. Engineering
2. Airlock
3. Dressing Room
4. Dressing/ Makeup Area
5. Stage
6. Prop Closet

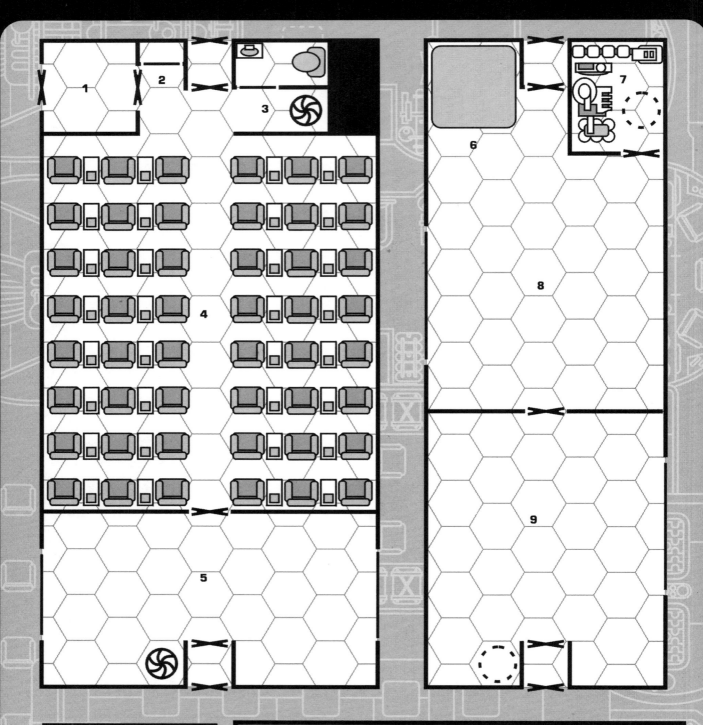

One hex equals one yard.

Symbol key on p. 65

1   2   3

LEGEND

1. Airlock
2. Suit Locker
3. Fresher
4. Seating
5. Cargo Bay
6. Vehicle Fuel Stores
7. Engineering and Life Support
8-9. Vehicle Bays

TUGBOAT CUTTER (TL10)

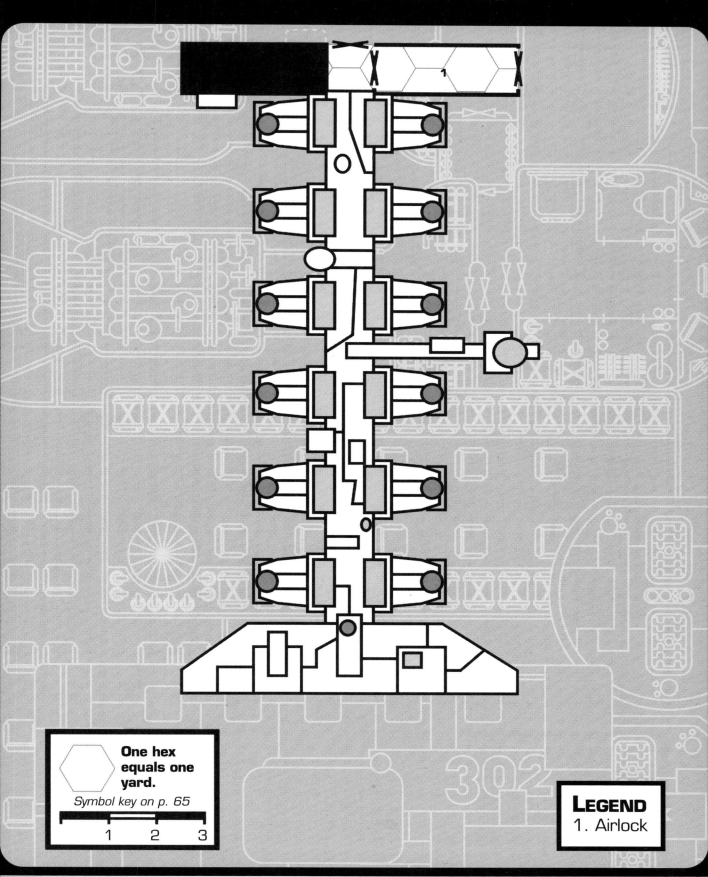

One hex equals one yard.

Symbol key on p. 65

1   2   3

LEGEND
1. Airlock

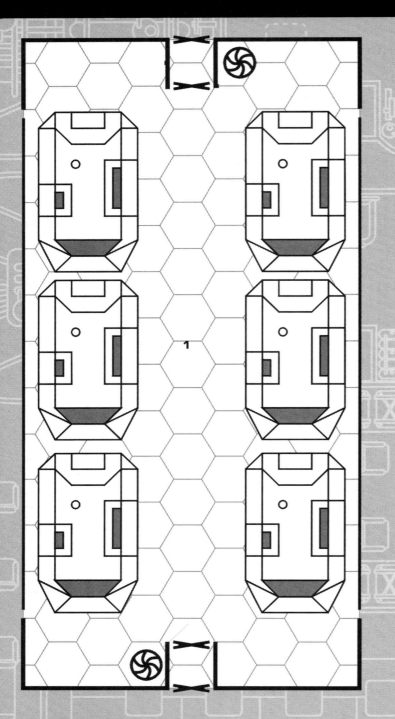

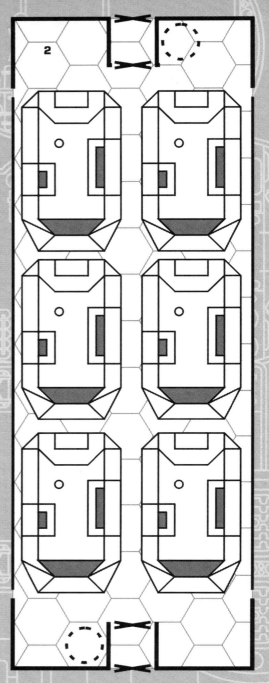

1

2

One hex equals one yard.

Symbol key on p. 65

1   2   3

LEGEND
1. Upper Vehicle Bay
2. Lower Vehicle Bay

WEAPONRY

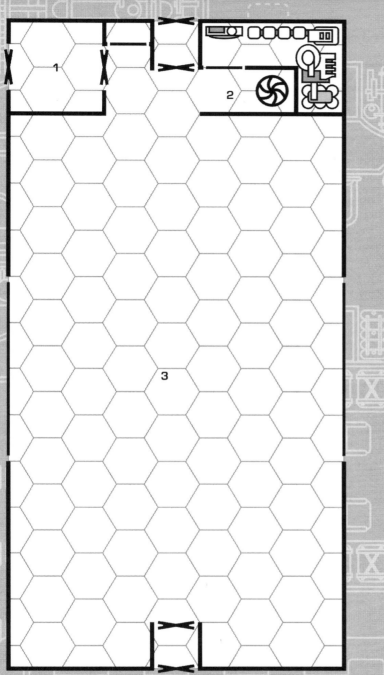

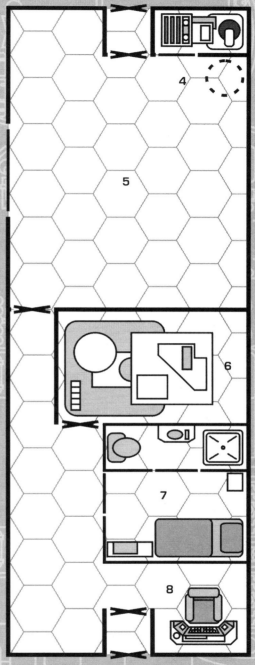

One hex equals one yard.

Symbol key on p. 65

1 2 3

LEGEND
1. Airlock
2. Engineering
3. Cargo Bay
4. Life Support
5. Magazine
6. Weaponry
7. Stateroom
8. Fire Control

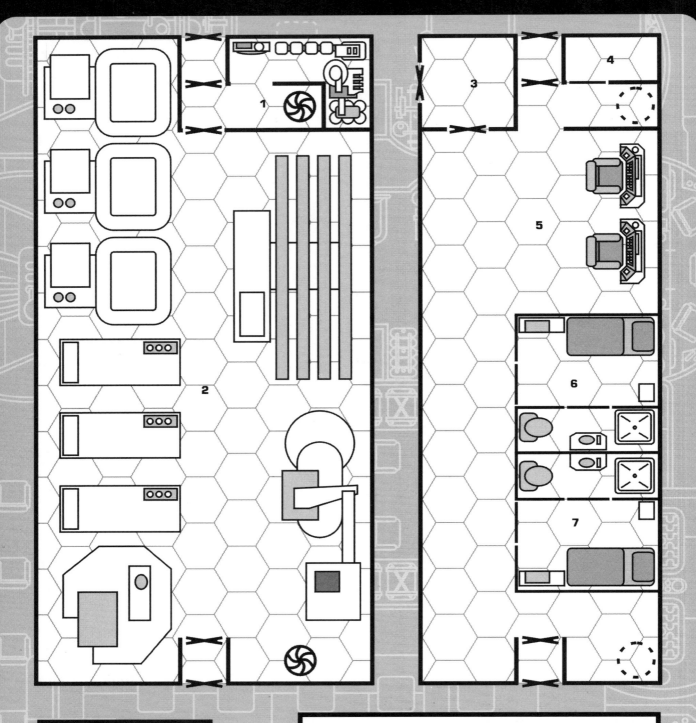

One hex equals one yard.

Symbol key on p. 65

1   2   3

Legend

1. Engineering
2. Communications Equipment Bay
3. Airlock
4. Closet
5. Communications Control
6-7. Stateroom

COMMAND STATION (TL10)

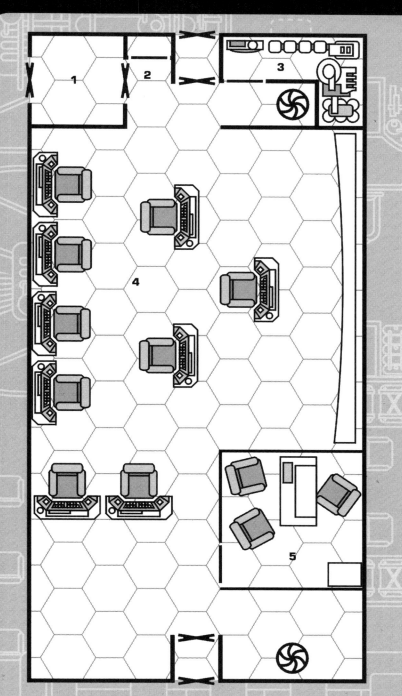

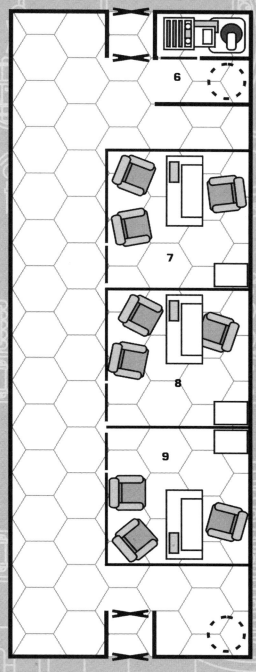

One hex equals one yard.

Symbol key on p. 65

1   2   3

LEGEND
1. Airlock
2. Suit Locker
3. Engineering

4. Command Center
5. Office
6. Life Support
7-9. Office

COMMERCIAL STATION (TL10)

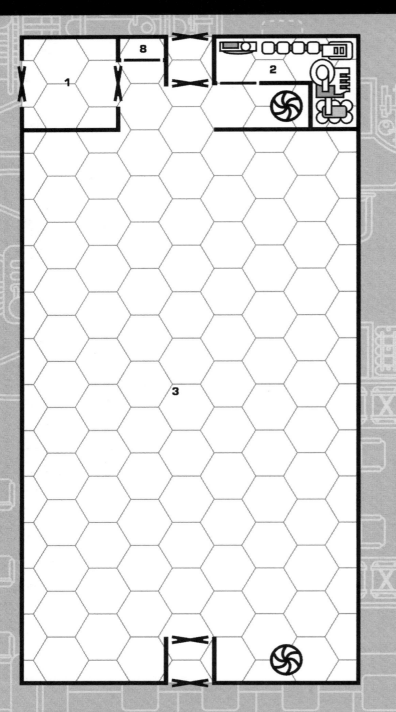

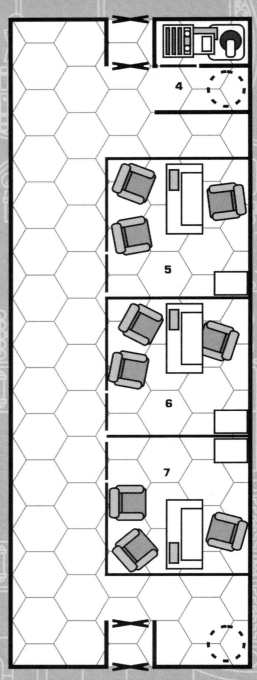

One hex equals one yard.

Symbol key on p. 65

1   2   3

LEGEND

1. Airlock
2. Engineering
3. Open Area
4. Life Support
5-7. Office
8. Suit Locker

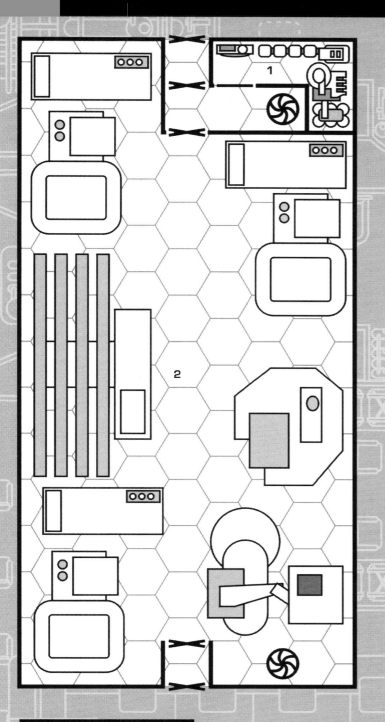

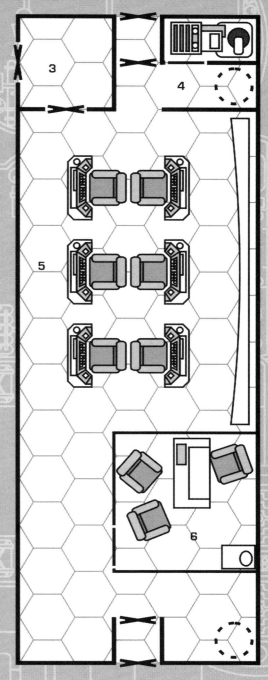

One hex equals one yard.

Symbol key on p. 65

1   2   3

LEGEND

1. Engineering
2. Communications Equipment Bay
3. Airlock
4. Life Support
5. Dispatch Center
6. Office

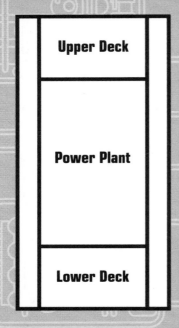

Upper Deck

Power Plant

Lower Deck

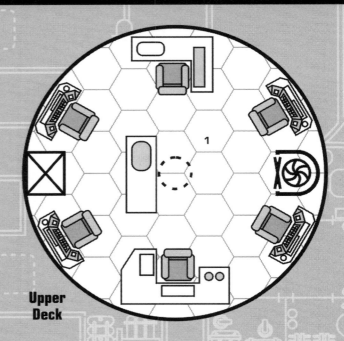

Upper Deck

1

Power Plant

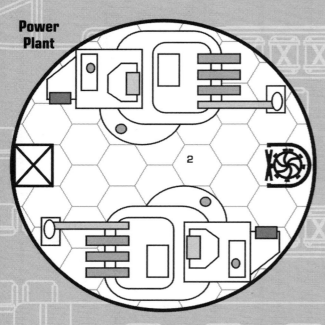

2

Lower Deck

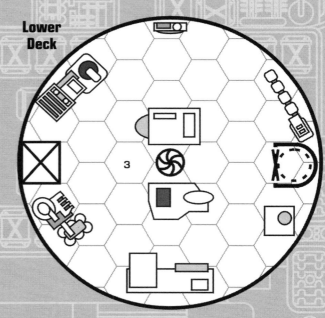

3

One hex equals one yard.

Symbol key on p. 65

1   2   3

Symbol key on p. 65

LEGEND
1. Control Center
2. Power Plant
3. Life Support/ Workshop

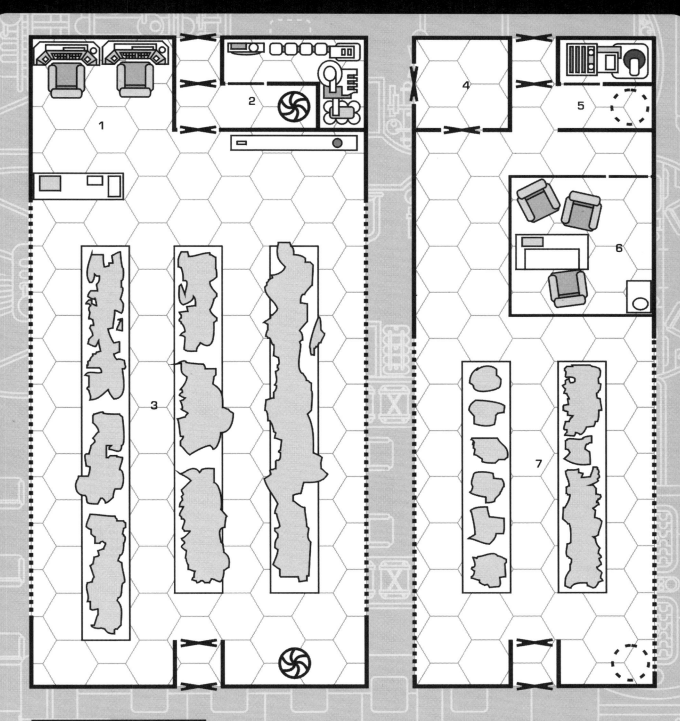

One hex equals one yard.

Symbol key on p. 65

1   2   3

LEGEND
1. Controls
2. Engineering
3. Plant Beds
4. Airlock
5. Life Support
6. Office
7. Plant Beds

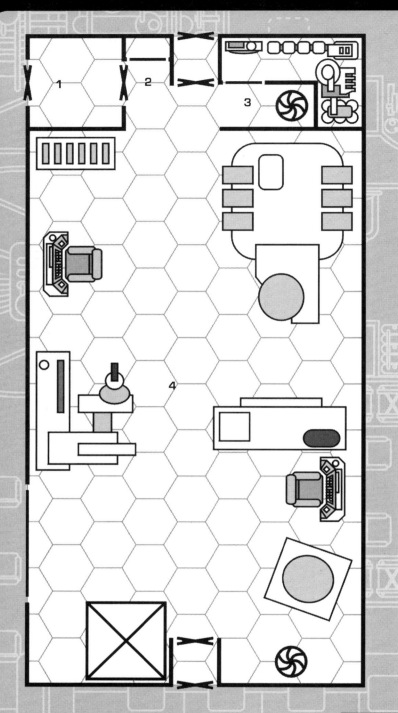

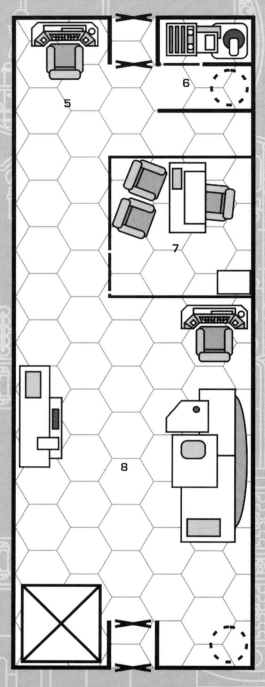

One hex equals one yard.

Symbol key on p. 65

1 2 3

LEGEND

1. Airlock
2. Suit Locker
3. Engineering
4. Workshop
5. Controls
6. Life Support
7. Office
8. Workshop

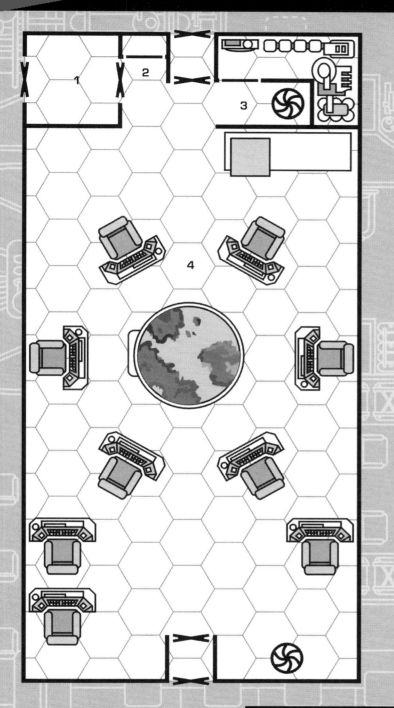

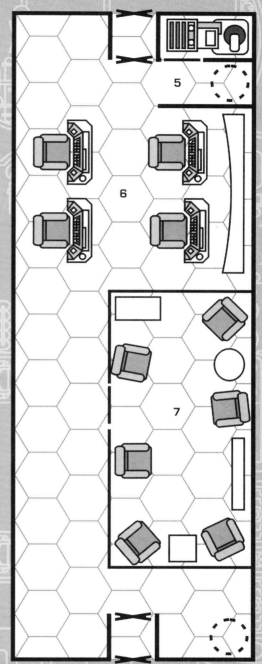

One hex
equals one
yard.

Symbol key on p. 65

1   2   3

LEGEND

1. Airlock
2. Suit Locker
3. Engineering
4. Flight-Traffic Control
5. Life Support
6. Communications Center
7. Lounge

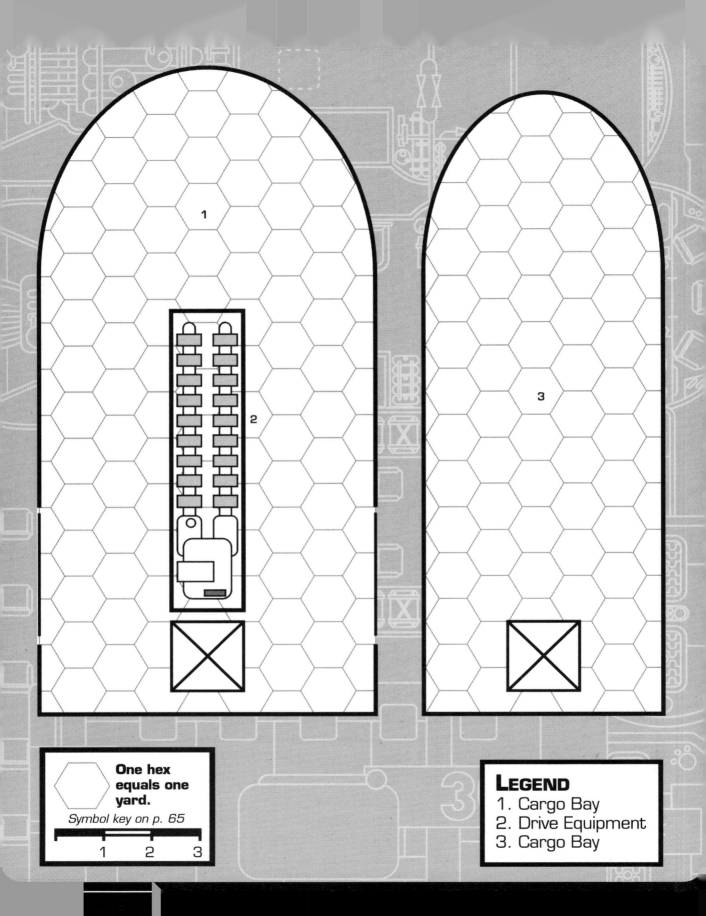

1

2

3

One hex
equals one
yard.

Symbol key on p. 65

1   2   3

LEGEND
1. Cargo Bay
2. Drive Equipment
3. Cargo Bay

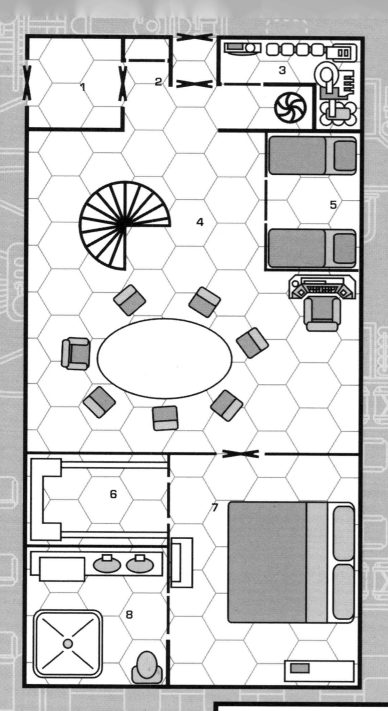
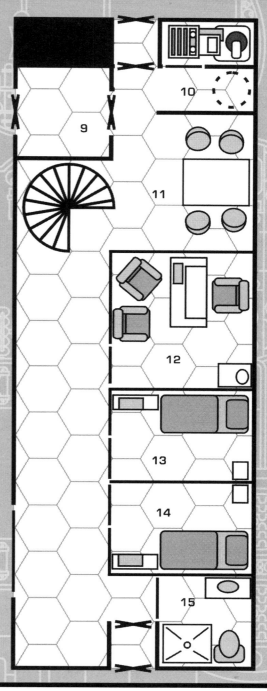

1
2
3
4
5
9
10
11
12
13
14
15
6
7
8

One hex equals one yard.

Symbol key on p. 65

1   2   3

LEGEND
1. Airlock
2. Suit Locker
3. Engineering
4. Conference Room
5. Sickbay
6. Closet
7. Master Bedroom
8. Bathroom
9. Airlock
10. Life Support
11. Break Area
12. Office
13-14. Staterooms
15. Fresher

The following chart shows the fully loaded performance ratings of the various modular small craft and the jump cutter.

Standard Modules

	Basic	Slow	Fast	Multi	Advanced	Assault	Stealth	Hiver	Jump
Boarding	–	–	–	–	2.6	2.8	3.4	–	1.0
Bulk Cargo	2.0	–	2.9	1.8	3.7	3.8	5.0	–	1.0
Cargo	2.2	1.6	3.2	2.0	4.0	4.0	5.4	–	1.1
Advanced	–	–	2.6	1.5	3.3	3.5	4.4	–	0.8
Armored	–	–	–	–	2.6	2.9	3.5	–	0.6
Stealth	2.0	–	2.9	1.8	3.7	3.8	5.0	–	1.0
Class I Starport	3.4	2.7	4.6	3.3	5.5	5.2	7.7	–	1.7
Commuter	3.8	3.1	5.0	3.7	6.0	5.5	8.4	–	1.9
Containerized Cargo	2.2	1.6	3.1	2.0	3.9	4.0	5.3	–	1.0
Customs	3.0	2.3	4.1	2.8	5.0	4.8	6.9	–	1.5
ECM	2.0	–	2.9	1.8	3.6	3.8	4.9	–	0.9
Expandable Base	2.5	1.9	3.5	2.3	4.4	4.3	6.0	–	1.2
Fast Courier	–	–	–	–	6.5	6.1	7.9	–	2.8
Fighter Pod	2.5	1.9	3.5	2.3	4.4	4.4	6.0	–	1.2
Advanced	–	–	2.5	1.5	3.2	3.4	4.3	–	0.8
Firefighting	–	–	–	–	–	2.4	–	–	–
Fuel Skimmer	3.7	3.0	4.9	3.6	5.9	5.4	8.2	–	1.9
Advanced	2.6	1.9	3.6	2.4	4.5	4.4	6.1	–	1.2
Armored	–	–	2.6	1.6	3.3	3.5	4.5	–	0.8
Stealth	3.2	2.5	4.3	3.0	5.2	5.0	7.3	–	1.6
Garage	2.5	1.9	3.5	2.3	4.4	4.4	6.0	–	1.2
Advanced	1.9	–	2.8	1.7	3.6	3.7	4.8	–	0.9
Armored	–	–	–	–	2.8	3.0	3.7	–	0.7
Stealth	2.2	1.7	3.2	2.0	4.0	4.1	5.5	–	1.1
High-Cap. Troop Berthing	3.1	2.4	4.2	2.9	5.2	4.9	7.2	–	1.5
Laboratory	2.8	2.1	3.9	2.6	4.8	4.7	6.6	–	1.4
Logistics	2.2	1.6	3.1	2.0	4.0	4.0	5.4	–	1.1
Lounge	3.8	3.1	5.0	3.7	6.0	5.5	8.5	–	1.9
Low Berth	2.5	1.9	3.6	2.3	4.5	4.4	6.1	–	1.2
Luxury Passenger	2.9	2.2	4.0	2.7	4.9	4.8	6.8	–	1.4
Luxury Quarters	3.4	2.7	4.6	3.3	5.6	5.2	7.8	–	1.7
Marine Command	–	–	–	–	2.7	2.9	3.6	–	0.6
Marine Firebase	–	–	–	–	2.7	2.9	3.5	–	0.6
Medevac	3.4	2.7	4.5	3.2	5.5	5.2	7.7	–	1.7
Medical	3.1	2.4	4.2	2.9	5.2	4.9	7.2	–	1.5
Mining	–	–	2.7	1.7	3.5	3.6	4.7	–	0.9
Nuclear Damper	–	–	–	–	2.7	2.9	3.6	–	0.6
Orbital Insertion	–	–	–	–	–	2.2	–	–	–
Passenger	2.4	1.8	3.4	2.2	4.3	4.3	5.8	–	1.2
Advanced	–	–	2.7	1.7	3.5	3.6	4.7	–	0.9
Armored	–	–	–	–	2.8	3.0	3.7	–	0.7
Stealth	2.2	1.6	3.1	2.0	3.9	4.0	5.3	–	1.0
Planetary Infrastructure	2.6	2.0	3.7	2.4	4.6	4.5	6.3	–	1.3
Portable Field Shop	2.7	2.1	3.8	2.5	4.7	4.6	6.5	–	1.3
Prison Transport	2.8	2.2	3.9	2.6	4.8	4.7	6.7	–	1.4
Quarters	3.5	2.8	4.7	3.4	5.6	5.3	7.9	–	1.8
Advanced	2.5	1.9	3.5	2.3	4.4	4.4	6.0	–	1.2
Armored	–	–	2.6	1.5	3.3	3.5	4.4	–	0.8
Stealth	3.1	2.4	4.2	2.9	5.1	4.9	7.1	–	1.5
Recovery	–	–	–	–	2.8	3.1	3.8	–	0.7
Recreation	4.5	3.8	5.7	4.5	6.7	6.0	9.5	–	2.3
Safari	3.0	2.3	4.1	2.8	5.0	4.8	6.9	–	1.5
Scout Support Base	2.7	2.0	3.7	2.5	4.6	4.5	6.3	–	1.3
Scout Survey Base	2.8	2.2	3.9	2.6	4.8	4.7	6.7	–	1.4
Search and Rescue	–	–	–	–	3.2	3.4	4.0	–	–
Sensor	–	–	2.6	1.5	3.3	3.4	4.4	–	0.8
Small Craft Bay	2.6	2.0	3.7	2.4	4.5	4.5	6.3	–	1.3
Standard Commercial	2.4	1.8	3.4	2.2	4.2	4.2	5.7	–	1.1
Survey	3.6	2.9	4.7	3.4	5.7	5.3	8.0	–	1.8
Theater	3.8	3.1	5.0	3.7	5.9	5.5	8.4	–	1.9
Traveling Stage	3.8	3.1	5.0	3.7	5.9	5.5	8.4	–	1.9
Troop Transport	2.3	1.7	3.3	2.1	4.1	4.1	5.6	–	1.1
Tugboat Cutter	–	–	–	–	2.5	2.8	3.4	–	0.6
Vehicle Transport	3.4	2.7	4.6	3.3	5.6	5.2	7.8	–	1.7
Xboat Relay	2.0	–	2.9	1.8	3.7	3.8	5.0	–	1.0
MagLev	2.2	1.7	3.2	2.0	4.0	4.1	5.5	–	1.1
Noble Transport	4.1	3.4	5.3	4.0	6.3	5.7	8.9	–	2.1

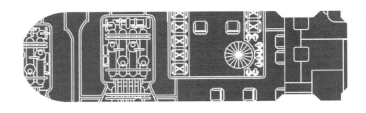

Weaponry Modules

	Basic	Slow	Fast	Multi	Advanced	Assault	Stealth	Hiver	Jump
Laser	2.1	–	3.0	1.9	3.8	3.9	5.2	–	1.0
Advanced	–	–	2.5	1.5	3.2	3.4	4.3	–	0.8
Energy	2.0	–	3.0	1.8	3.7	3.8	5.1	–	1.0
Advanced	–	–	2.5	1.5	3.2	3.4	4.3	–	0.8
Armored	–	–	–	–	2.6	2.8	3.4	–	0.6
Missile	2.1	–	3.1	1.9	3.8	3.9	5.2	–	1.0
Advanced	–	–	2.4	1.4	3.1	3.3	4.1	–	0.8
Armored	–	–	–	–	2.5	2.7	3.3	–	–
Sandcaster	2.2	1.6	3.2	2.0	4.0	4.0	5.4	–	1.1
Advanced	–	–	2.6	1.6	3.3	3.5	4.4	–	0.8

Station Modules

	Basic	Slow	Fast	Multi	Advanced	Assault	Stealth	Hiver	Jump
Command	3.1	2.4	4.2	2.9	5.2	4.9	7.2	–	1.5
Commercial	3.8	3.1	5.0	3.7	6.0	5.5	8.5	–	1.9
Communications	–	–	2.7	1.6	3.4	3.6	4.6	–	0.9
Engineering	2.4	1.8	3.5	2.2	4.3	4.3	5.9	–	1.2
Hydroponics	2.3	1.7	3.3	2.1	4.1	4.2	5.6	–	1.1
Industrial	2.2	1.6	3.2	2.0	4.0	4.1	5.4	–	1.1
Traffic Control	3.0	2.3	4.1	2.8	5.0	4.8	6.9	–	1.5

Hiver Modules

	Basic	Slow	Fast	Multi	Advanced	Assault	Stealth	Hiver	Jump
Hiver Cargo	2.1	–	3.0	1.9	3.8	3.9	5.2	–	1.0
Hiver Embassy	2.8	2.2	3.9	2.6	4.8	4.7	6.7	3.4	1.4
Hiver Passenger	2.4	1.8	3.4	2.2	4.2	4.2	5.8	2.9	1.1
Hiver War	1.9	–	2.8	1.7	3.6	3.7	4.8	–	0.9